Real Estate wealth building

Your roadmap to financial freedom

By

Travis k.bone

Disclaimer Notice

Legal Notice

Disclaimer

Table of contents

BONUS #5: EFFECTIVE FOLLOW-UP METHOD & SCRIPTS FOR REALTORS

PROLOGUE

What if I told you that you could make millions of dollars in real estate, doing
nothing but sitting on a beach?
Piña coladas, little white umbrellas, endless sand sounds pretty great, right?
Well, that is not going to happen, at least not anytime soon. If you were looking
for an easy path to riches, rental properties are probably not the right avenue for
you. I know I've probably just lost half of those who picked up this book, and
that's okay. I know that millions more are willing to do what is necessary to find
success, even if that path is more difficult than the late night television
infomercials would have you believe.
Obviously, people flock to real estate for a reason. In my opinion, real estate can
provide the best, safest, fastest path to financial freedom compared with any

other method used to build wealth. I've seen it in my own life, which I'll explain
in a moment. But first, let's talk about what this book will not teach you.
If you were looking for a book written by the latest guru, you are going to be
disappointed. You are not going to learn some secret strategy that I discovered
and that no one else knows. After all, I'm not anything special. In fact, I'm just
like you. I may be further along on my real estate journey than you are, or I may
be years behind you in which case, I hope to learn from you as well. The truth
is that we're on the same journey together, playing the greatest game ever
invented. In writing this book, I hope to share with you the lessons I've learned
so far, both the successes and the mistakes. I believe these lessons will help you achieve a greater life than you have ever imagined.
Moreover, you should never learn from just one person, I believe, and anyone
who says otherwise is probably trying to sell you something. The best education
comes from experience, and by learning from the collective experiences of
others, you can supercharge your real estate ambitions to find greater success,
faster and with less drama.

Therefore, in the pages of this book I've incorporated the lessons and stories of
real estate investors from the BiggerPockets community in an effort to help you gain the greatest perspective. Together, as a community, let's help each other find financial freedom through real estate investing.

What Do You Want?

Let me ask you a very basic question: what do you want?
Go ahead, say it out loud. Money? A new house? To fire yor boss, quit your
job, and work for yourself? How about a better retirement? More wealth for your
kids? A summer Europe? Longer sleep? Whatever it is, yell it out! (Unless
you are sitting in a Starbucks right now, in which case, you probably shouldn't
yell. But I'd like a tall extra-hot peppermint hot chocolate, please!) Let me share
with you one my all-time favorite quotes. Michael Jordan (yes, that Michael
Jordan) once said, "Some people want it to happen. Some wish it would happen.
Others make it happen."
Which kind of person are you?
Now, there is nothing wrong with wanting things in life. Don't feel silly about
identifying material things you want when you answer that question. Having
goals is great but it's not enough! You need action, too! You will need to get
off your butt and change your world yourself, because no one else will do it for
you. My goal in writing this book is to not only give you theory and hope but to

also give you the tools and knowledge you need to reach your goals. You
already know that real estate can change your life. Now it's time to leam how to
make that happen. It's time to take action.

- Are you committed to taking action?
- Are you committed to dedicating your spare time?
- Are you committed to replacing daydreams with strategies?
- Are you committed to investing your money?

I hope you answered "yes" to all of these questions. And don't worry if you
don't actually have the money, the spare time, or the knowledge just yet. If you
are committed to giving this a try, I'll help you get there. Remember, you are not
doing this for me; you are doing it for you.

As you work through this book, I encourage you to not only read but also
internalize every concept. Don't simply pass your eyes over the words without
understanding the concepts being explained. Reread sections if you need to. Ask other experienced investors about the topics. Share the lessons you're learning
with your significant other as you digest them. Question everything I say, and do
whatever is necessary to have it make sense in your own mind. Take your time.

About This Book

This book will likely ruin your life, as great books tend to do.
It will challenge the way you look at life, finances, and real estate. It will lead
you to envision a different life for yourself, one not suggested by your parents,
society, your alma mater, or the media. It will encourage you to step out and
create a whole new path for yourself, one that you construct out of thin air. It
will introduce you to numerous ideas, paths, and concepts for
achieving financial freedom through rental properties. It will give you answers to
questions you never knew to ask, and likely leave you with a few more questions
I didn't think to answer (but don't worry, that's not a bad thing).
My goal with this book is to create the single greatest guide on rental property
investing ever written. Trust me , I've read hundreds! In each chapter, I will
explore one specific step in rental property investing, explaining it in depth and
helping you understand how to navigate every stage of the process.

Whether you are just getting started or already own hundreds of units, I hope this
book will help you make more income, retire sooner, unlock more free time,
amass more units, or achieve whatever other goals you might have. Yes, this is
an ambitious undertaking, but I am up for the challenge. Are you?

Finally, I believe one pass through this book will not be enough. I include so
many lessons, tips, stories, and details that you'll likely remember only 209% of
what you read. Do you want to be only 20% prepared to take on your first (or
next) rental property investment? I didn't think so! I therefore encourage you to
read this entire book not just once but multiple times. You'll never look back at
your life and say, I sure wish I hadn't spent so much time preparing for my
future." As good ole Abe Lincoln reportedly remarked, "Give me six hours to
chop down a tree, and I will spend the first four sharpening the axe."

Ir's time to sharpen your axe. I'll see you in Chapter 1.

Your friend,

Travis k.bone.

INTRODUCTION

Real estate is one of the most dynamic and complex industries in the world, with a rich history and a constantly evolving landscape. From residential homes to commercial properties, from small towns to global metropolises, real estate touches nearly every aspect of our lives, driving economic growth, shaping communities, and providing a foundation for both personal and professional success. At its core, real estate is all about the art and science of property transactions, where buyers and sellers, landlords, and tenants, investors and developers, come together to create value and opportunity. But it is also much more than that - it is about understanding the fundamental forces that shape the demand for and supply of property, from demographic trends and economic cycles to technological advances and environmental concerns. This book is designed to be a comprehensive guide to the world of real estate, covering both the theoretical and practical aspects of the industry. We will explore topics
such as property rights, land use regulations, financing options, investment strategies, and the legal and financial implications of various types of real estate transactions. We
will also delve into the essential skills and traits that are required for success in the industry, including communication, negotiation, problem- solving, and

Relationship-Building. But our exploration of real estate doesn't end there. We will also examine the broader social and

the economic impact of real estate, including its role in shaping communities, creating jobs, and

driving economic growth. We will consider issues such as affordable housing, sustainable development, and equitable access to resources, and offer strategies for addressing

these challenges in a responsible and ethical manner. Whether you are a seasoned real estate professional looking to deepen your understanding of the industry, or a newcomer seeking to gain a foothold in this exciting and dynamic field, this book will be an invaluable

resource. With its comprehensive coverage, practical insights, and deep understanding the nuances of the industry, it will provide you with the knowledge and skills needed to

succeed in the world of real estate. So come along with us on this journey of discovery and exploration, as we navigate the ever-changing landscape of real estate and discover the secrets to success in this fascinating and rewarding industry.

CHAPTER ONE

<u>THE BEGINNING OF YOUR JOURNEY.</u>

Real estate is a complex and a multifaceted industry that requires a unique set of skills and expertise to succeed. In chapter one of this book, we'll explore the beginning of your journey into the world of real estate, equipping you with the foundational knowledge and tools needed to navigate this dynamic field with confidence and competence.

In this chapter, we'll delve into the foundational principles that underpin Success in the world of real estate, providing you with a comprehensive understanding of the industry's ins and outs. From exploring the different types of real estate Investments and understanding the market forces that drive them, to develop a strategic investment plan and building a strong
team of professionals to support you, we'll guide you through every step of the process.

Through real-world case studies and practical advice from seasoned experts in the field, you'll gain a deeper understanding of the risks and rewards of real estate investing, and learn how to leverage them to your advantage. We'll also explore the importance of cultivating a growth mindset and a willingness to learn, adapt, and evolve in response to changing market conditions and emerging trends.

Through a comprehensive analysis of the real estate landscape, we'll delve into the essential concepts and principles that underpin success in this industry. From understanding the
various types of real estate investments and financing options available, to develop a keen sense of market analysis and identifying profitable opportunities, you'll gain a comprehensive understanding of the fundamentals of real estate.

We'll also examine the critical legal and regulatory frameworks that
govern the industry, ensuring that you're well-versed in the laws and regulations that affect real estate transactions. Additionally, we'll provide you with strategies for building strong relationships with clients and stakeholders, honing your negotiation skills, and developing a
winning mindset that will set you apart from your competitors.

But real estate is about more than just transactions and paperwork - it'salso, a people-driven industry that requires strong communication, negotiation, and interpersonal skills.
That's why we'll also focus on the importance of building relationships
and fostering trust with clients, colleagues, and other stakeholders in the real estate ecosystem.

Finally, we'll explore some of the common challenges and pitfalls that real estate professionals face, and provide you with strategies for overcoming these obstacles and thriving in this competitive and constantly evolving field. From managing risk and navigating the market fluctuations to staying up-to-date with the latest technologies and trends, we'll equip you with the tools and insights needed to stay ahead of the curve and succeed in real estate.

By the end of this chapter, you'll be equipped with the tools and insights needed to lay a strong foundation for your real estate career. Whether you're a seasoned professional or a newcomer to the industry, this book will serve as your ultimate guide and companion on your journey towards real estate success. So get ready to take your first steps into the exciting World of real estate, and let's start building your path to prosperity together

Summary of chapter one

- Real estate industry requires unique skills and expertise to succeed.
- Chapter one of the book focuses on equipping the reader with foundational
- knowledge and tools to navigate the real estate field with confidence and Competence.
- The chapter covers various aspects such as real estate investments, market analysis, legal and regulatory frameworks, and building strong relationships.
- The importance of a growth mindset, willingness to learn, adapt and evolve is emphasized.
- The chapter provides strategies for overcoming challenges and pitfalls faced by real estate professionals and staying ahead of the curve.
- The book serves as an ultimate guide and companion for both seasoned professionals and newcomers to the industry.

CHAPTER TWO

The Essential Tools of the Trade: Technology and Resources for Real Estate Success

In the modern era of real estate, technology has become an essential tool for success. From digital

marketing to virtual tours, technology has revolutionized the way real estate professionals conduct business and interact with clients. But with so many tools and resources available, it can be overwhelming to know where to begin. The first step to success is to understand the essential tools of the trade. This includes having a strong online presence, utilizing customer relationship management (CRM) software, and leveraging social media
platforms to connect with potential clients. A professional website that showcases your listings and expertise is also crucial in today's digital landscape. Another key tool for success is virtual
tours, which allow prospective buyers to view properties from the comfort of their own homes. This technology has become even more important in the wake of the COVID-19 pandemic, as many buyers are hesitant to attend in-person showings. In addition to technology, there is a
variety of resources that can help real estate professionals achieve success. Professional associations, such as the National Association of Realtors offer training, support, and networking opportunities. Real Estate coaches and mentors can provide valuable guidance and insight, while industry publications and blogs can help you stay up-to-date on the latest
trends and developments in the industry.Ultimately, success in real estate requires a combination of both technology and human connection. While technology can streamline

processes and help you reach a wider audience, it's important to remember
that real estate is a people-centric business. Building and nurturing relationships with clients, colleagues, and other industry professionals are essential for long-term success.By understanding and utilizing the essential tools of the trade, real estate professionals can achieve success in today's fast-paced and ever-changing industry. Whether you're a seasoned veteran or just starting, investing in technology and resources can help you build a thriving and rewarding real estate business.

Developing Your Business Plan: A Strategic Approach to Real Estate Success

Developing a solid business plan is essential for achieving success in the competitive world of real estate. A business plan provides a roadmap for your real estate business, outlining your goals, strategies, and action plans for achieving success. A

strategic approach to developing your business plan is crucial for ensuring that you're setting realistic goals, utilizing your resources effectively, and maximizing your potential for growth and profitability. The first step in developing a business plan is to identify your goals. This could include setting financial targets, establishing a niche market, or expanding your client base. Once you have established your goals, you can begin to develop a strategy for achieving them. This may involve identifying your target market determining the services you'll offer, and creating a marketing plan to reach your audience. Your business plan should also

include an analysis of your strengths, weaknesses, opportunities, and threats (SWOT). This will help you identify areas where you excel and where you need to improve, as well as potential challenges and opportunities in the market. Financial planning is also a critical

component of any business plan. This may include developing a budget, forecasting revenue and expenses, and establishing financial goals for your business. It's important to regularly review and adjust your financial plan to ensure that you're staying on track and making informed decisions. Another important aspect of developing a business plan is creating an action plan for achieving your goals. This may involve setting specific tasks and timeliness, delegating

responsibilities to the team members, and establishing key performance indicators (KPIs) to
measure your progress.
Finally, it's important to regularly review and update your business plan
as your business evolves. This may involve adjusting your goals, strategies, and action plans based on changing market conditions or new
opportunities. By developing a strategic and comprehensive business plan, real estate professionals can establish a strong foundation for success. A well-crafted business plan can help you stay focused, make informed decisions, and achieve your goals, even in the face of challenges and competition. With a clear vision and a strategic approach, real estate professionals can a thriving and profitable business in the dynamic and ever-changing world of real estate

Finding Your Niche: Specializing and Standing Out in a Competitive Market

In today's fast-paced and ever-evolving world, finding your niche and specializing in
a particular field is not only important but necessary for success in a highly
competitive market. With so many businesses and individuals vying for attention
and market share, it's essential to stand out from the crowd and establish yourself
as an expert in your field.
One of the key benefits of finding your niche is that it allows you to focus your
efforts and resources on a specific area of expertise. This, in turn, enables you to
build your skills and knowledge in that area and become an authority in your field.
By specializing, you can provide a more targeted and valuable service to your
clients or customers, which can lead to increased demand for your services and
higher profits.
However, finding your niche is not always easy. It requires a deep understanding of
your strengths, passions, and unique qualities, as well as market research and

analysis to identify gaps or opportunities in the market. It also requires a
willingness to take risks, experiment, and adapt to changing market conditions.
Once you have identified your niche and established yourself as an expert in your
field, the next step is to stand out from the competition. This requires a strategic
approach to branding, marketing, and networking, as well as a commitment to
providing exceptional service and quality to your clients or customers.
Building a strong personal brand is key to standing out in a competitive market.
Your brand should reflect your values, expertise, and unique selling proposition,
and be consistent across all channels, including social media, website, and offline
marketing materials. A well-defined brand can help you attract the right clients or
customers and differentiate yourself from competitors.
Marketing and networking are also crucial to standing out in a competitive market.
This involves identifying your target audience and developing a targeted marketing
strategy that reaches them through various channels, such as social media, email
marketing, and advertising. Building strong relationships with other professionals
in your industry through networking can also help you gain referrals and build your

reputation.

In conclusion, finding your niche and specializing in a particular field is essential for success in a competitive market. By focusing your efforts and resources on a specific area of expertise, building your skills and knowledge, and establishing yourself as an expert, you can provide a more targeted and valuable service to your clients or customers, leading to increased demand and higher profits. Standing out from the competition requires a strategic approach to branding, marketing, and networking, as well as a commitment to providing exceptional service and quality.

Building Your Network: Relationship-Building and

Networking Strategies for Real Estate Success

In the real estate industry, building a strong network is essential for success. A
robust network of contacts and relationships can help you generate leads, find
new clients, and secure deals that would otherwise be out of reach. However,
building a network takes time and effort, and it requires a strategic approach to
relationship-building and networking.
One of the most important strategies for building your network is to prioritize
relationship-building. This means focusing on building genuine connections with
people rather than simply collecting business cards or adding contacts on
LinkedIn. By taking the time to get to know people, understanding their needs and
interests, and finding ways to add value to their lives or businesses, you can
establish strong, long-lasting relationships that can benefit both parties.
Another key strategy for building your network is to diversify your contacts and
relationships. This means seeking out people from a variety of industries,

backgrounds, and demographics. By broadening your network, you can tap into
new markets, find new opportunities, and gain different perspectives on the real
estate industry. It's also important to engage with people at all levels of the
industry, from seasoned professionals to up-and-coming agents and brokers.
Networking events and conferences can be valuable opportunities for building
your network, but it's important to approach these events strategically. Rather than
trying to meet as many people as possible, focus on building meaningful
connections with a few key individuals. Research the attendees in advance,
identify people you want to connect with and come prepared with thoughtful
questions and talking points. After the event, follow up with your new contacts and
find ways to stay in touch and continue building your relationship.
Social media can also be a powerful tool for building your network. Linkedin, in
particular, is a valuable platform for connecting with other real estates
professionals, sharing industry news and insights, and building your personal
brand. It's important to approach social media with a strategic plan and to

consistently engage with your connections by commenting on posts, sharing
content, and reaching out to new contacts.
In conclusion, building your network is essential for success in the real estate
industry. By prioritizing relationship-building, diversifying your contacts and
relationships, attending networking events strategically, and leveraging social
media, you can build a robust network of contacts and relationships that can help
you achieve your professional goals. Remember, building a network takes time and
effort, but the rewards can be significant in terms of generating leads, finding new
clients, and securing deals.

Managing Your Finances: Budgeting, Accounting, and Investment Strategies for Real Estate Professionals

As a real estate professional, managing your finances effectively is essential for

long-term success. This requires a solid understanding of budgeting, accounting,
and investment strategies, as well as a commitment to staying on top of your
financial situation at all times.
One of the most important aspects of managing your finances is creating a
budget. A budget helps you keep track of your income and expenses, identify
areas where you can cut costs or increase revenue, and plan for the future. To
create an effective budget, it's important to track your expenses and income
accurately, prioritize your spending, and review your budget regularly to make
adjustments as needed.
Accounting is another critical component of financial management. Keeping
accurate and up-to-date financial records can help you make informed decisions
about your business and identify potential areas for growth. This may involve
working with a professional accountant or using accounting software to manage
your finances efficiently.
Investment strategies are also important for real estate professionals. This may
involve investing in real estate properties, stocks, bonds, or other assets. It's
important to approach investments strategically, considering factors such as risk

tolerance, return on investment, and diversification. Working with a financial
advisor can help you develop an investment strategy that aligns with your financial
goals and risk profile.

In addition to these core strategies, other financial management
practices can help real estate professionals succeed. For example,
establishing an emergency fund can provide a safety net in case of unexpected
expenses or a downturn in the market. Developing a debt reduction plan can help
you pay off loans and credit cards efficiently, freeing up cash flow for other
investments or expenses.

Ultimately, managing your finances effectively requires discipline, focus, and a
commitment to staying on top of your financial situation. By developing a solid
budget, keeping accurate financial records, investing strategically, and practicing
other financial management strategies, you can set yourself up for long-term
success in the real estate industry. Remember, financial management is an
ongoing process, and it's important to review your strategies and adjust your
approach as needed to achieve your goals.

Marketing Your Brand: Creating a Strong and Memorable Brand Identity for Real Estate

In the competitive world of real estate, creating a strong and memorable brand
Identity is essential for success. A strong brand identity can help you stand out
from the competition, build trust with clients, and establish a reputation for
excellence. However, building a brand identity requires a thoughtful and strategic
approach.
One of the first steps in creating a strong brand identity is defining your brand
values and mission. This involves identifying what sets you apart from other real
estate professionals and what values guide your work. By articulating your brand
values clearly, you can develop a brand identity that resonates with your target
audience and helps you establish a unique position in the market.

Another key component of building a brand identity is creating a memorable visual
identity. This may include developing a logo, color scheme, and other visual
elements that communicate your brand values and mission. It's important to
ensure that your visual identity is consistent across all channels, from your
website and social media profiles to your business cards and marketing materials.
Developing a strong online presence is also critical for building your brand identity.
This may involve creating a website that showcases your expertise, sharing
valuable content on social media, and engaging with your audience through email
marketing and other digital channels. By establishing a strong online presence, you
can expand your reach and connect with potential clients more effectively.
In addition to these core strategies, other tactics can help you build a
strong and memorable brand identity. For example, developing a unique selling
proposition (USP) can help you differentiate yourself from other real estate
professionals and communicate the unique value you offer. Hosting events or
webinars can also help you build your brand and establish yourself as a thought
leader in the industry.

Ultimately, building a strong and memorable brand identity requires a combination
of strategic thinking, creativity, and hard work. By defining your brand values and
mission, creating a memorable visual identity, developing a strong online presence,
and engaging in other branding tactics, you can establish yourself as a trusted and
respected real estate professional. Remember, building a brand identity is an
ongoing process, and it's important to continue refining your approach to achieve
your goals.

Developing Your Sales Skills: Techniques and Strategies for Effective Real Estate Sales

As a real estate professional, your success depends on your ability to close deals
and generate revenue. Developing your sales skills is essential for achieving your
goals and building a thriving real estate business. However, effective real estate
sales require a combination of strategies and techniques that can take time to

master.

One of the first steps in developing your sales skills is understanding your target
audience. This involves researching your market, identifying potential clients, and
understanding their needs and preferences. By understanding your audience, you
can tailor your sales approach to meet their unique needs and build trust and
rapport with them.

Another important aspect of effective real estate sales is building relationships
with potential clients. This involves actively networking, engaging with prospects,
and establishing yourself as a reliable and knowledgeable resource in the industry.
By building relationships with potential clients, you can establish trust and
increase the likelihood of closing deals.

In addition to relationship-building, there are several sales techniques and
strategies that can help you close deals more effectively. For example, developing
a strong value proposition can help you communicate the unique value you offer
and differentiate yourself from other real estate professionals. Using persuasive
language and effective storytelling can also help you connect with clients and
inspire them to take action.

Another key aspect of effective real estate sales is understanding the buying
process and the emotions that drive it. By understanding the psychology of buying
and the factors that influence decision-making, you can develop more effective
sales strategies and close deals more consistently. Ultimately, developing your sales skills requires a combination of practice,
persistence, and ongoing learning. By staying up-to-date with industry trends,
learning from successful sales professionals, and continuously refining your
approach, you can become a more effective and successful real estate
salesperson. Remember, effective sales is about building relationships,
understanding your audience, and communicating value in a way that inspires
action. By mastering these skills and strategies, you can achieve your goals and
build a thriving real estate business.

Staying Up-to-Date: Continuing Education and Professional Development for Real Estate Success

As a real estate professional, staying up-to-date with industry trends and best
practices is essential for achieving long-term success. The real estate industry is
constantly evolving, and keeping pace with changes in technology, regulations, and
consumer behavior is critical for maintaining a competitive edge.

One of the best ways to stay up-to-date with industry trends and best practices is
by investing in continuing education and professional development. This may
involve attending conferences, workshops, and seminars, taking online courses or
webinars, and participating in industry associations and organizations.

Continuing education can help you stay informed about changes in regulations,
legal requirements, and best practices in the industry. By staying up-to-date with

these changes, you can ensure that you are operating your business in compliance
with the law and delivering high-quality service to your clients.
Professional development can also help you hone your skills, learn new techniques
and strategies, and stay ahead of the competition. By investing in your
professional development, you can become a more effective and knowledgeable
real estate professional and build a reputation as a trusted expert in the industry.
In addition to formal continuing education and professional development, there are
other ways to stay up-to-date with industry trends and best practices. For example,
reading industry publications and blogs, following influential thought leaders on
social media, and attending networking events can all help you stay informed and
connected with other professionals in the industry.
Ultimately, staying up-to-date with industry trends and best practices requires a
commitment to ongoing learning and professional development. By investing in
your education and development, you can stay ahead of the competition,
provide high-quality service to your clients, and build a successful real estate
business. Remember, the real estate industry is constantly evolving, and staying

up-to-date is essential for achieving long-term success.

Balancing Work and Life: Strategies for Achieving Work-Life Balance in Real Estate
As a real estate professional, achieving a work-life balance can be a challenge. The
fast-paced and often unpredictable nature of the industry can make it difficult to
set boundaries and maintain a healthy work-life balance. However, finding
a balance between work and life is essential for maintaining your health and
wellbeing, as well as your long-term success in the industry.
One of the first steps in achieving work-life balance is setting clear boundaries
between work and personal time. This may involve setting specific work hours,
scheduling time for self-care and relaxation, and avoiding the temptation to check
work emails or take phone calls during personal time.
Another important strategy for achieving work-life balance is prioritizing your time
and focusing on the most important tasks first. This involves identifying your top
priorities, setting realistic goals, and avoiding distractions that can derail your
productivity.

In addition to setting boundaries and prioritizing your time, it is important to take
care of your physical and mental health. This may involve incorporating regular
exercise, healthy eating habits, and stress-reducing activities like meditation or
yoga into your routine. Taking care of your health and well-being can help you stay
focused, energized, and resilient in the face of the demands of the real estate
industry.

Finally, seeking support and accountability can be a powerful tool in achieving
work-life balance. This may involve working with a mentor or coach, joining a peer
support group, or seeking out resources and tools to help you manage your time
and stay focused on your priorities.

Ultimately, achieving work-life balance requires a commitment to setting clear
boundaries, prioritizing your time, taking care of your health and well-being, and
seeking support when needed. By finding a balance between work and life, you can
achieve greater happiness, fulfillment, and long-term success in the real estate
industry. Remember, taking care of yourself is essential for taking care of your
clients and building a thriving real estate business.

Overcoming Challenges: Dealing with Difficult Clients, Navigating Legal and Regulatory Issues, and Other Common Challenges in Real Estate

The real estate industry is fraught with challenges, and as a professional in the
field, you are likely to encounter a variety of difficulties throughout your career.
Whether you are dealing with difficult clients, navigating complex legal and
regulatory issues, or facing other common challenges in the industry, it is
important to have the skills and strategies necessary to overcome these obstacles
and continue to thrive.

One of the most common challenges in real estate is dealing with difficult clients.
This may involve managing unrealistic expectations, addressing disagreements,
and maintaining clear and effective communication throughout the transaction
process. To overcome these challenges, it is important to develop strong
communication skills, set clear boundaries, and remain patient and professional
even in the face of difficult situations.
Navigating legal and regulatory issues can also be a significant challenge in real
estate. From zoning and land use regulations to contract disputes and liability
issues, the legal landscape in real estate can be complex and ever-changing. To
navigate these challenges, it is important to stay up-to-date with changes in the
law, work with qualified legal professionals, and maintain meticulous records and
documentation throughout the transaction process.
Other common challenges in the real estate industry may include managing a
fluctuating market, dealing with unexpected delays or setbacks, and maintaining a
healthy work life balance. To overcome these challenges, it is important to remain
adaptable and flexible, seek out support and resources when needed, and prioritize
your physical and mental health and well-being.

Ultimately, overcoming challenges in real estate requires a combination of skills,
strategies, and resources. By developing strong communication skills, staying up-
to date with changes in the law, seeking out support and resources when needed,
and prioritizing your health and well-being, you can overcome the obstacles
that comes your way and continue to thrive in this challenging and rewarding
industry. Remember, every challenge is an opportunity for growth and learning, and
with the right mindset and approach, you can overcome even the toughest
obstacles and achieve long-term success in real estate.

CHAPTER THREE

BUILDING YOUR SOCIAL MEDIA AND BUSINESS PRESENCE: Establishing Your Social Media Presence: Tips for Beginners

Social media has become an integral part of modern-day marketing and business
practices, and as a beginner, it can be overwhelming to navigate through the vast
and the ever-evolving landscape of social media platforms. However, with the right
guidance and strategies, you can establish a strong online presence and build a
loyal following that will not only help you grow your business but also increase
brand awareness.

To get started with social media, it's crucial to define your social media strategy
and establish your online identity. This involves identifying your target audience,

choosing the right social media platforms that align with your business goals, and
creating compelling content that engages your audience and builds relationships.
It's also essential to understand the inner workings of social media algorithms and
how to use them to your advantage to increase your reach and engagement.
Posting regularly and sharing valuable content that resonates with your audience
is a critical aspect of building your following on social media. It's important to
determine the optimal frequency of posting and to share content that is not only
visually appealing but also provides value to your audience. Interacting with your
followers through comments, messages, and live videos can also help you build
relationships and establish trust.
Social media can also be an effective tool for driving traffic to your website and
generating leads. By incorporating call-to-actions and sharing relevant content that
leads back to your website, you can increase the chances of converting your
followers into customers.
Finally, measuring the success of your social media efforts through various tools
and metrics can help you track your progress and identify areas that need

improvement. This can help you refine your social media strategy and optimize
your efforts for maximum results.
In summary, establishing your social media presence and building your business
online requires a combination of strategy, creativity, and consistency. By following
these tips and best practices, you can successfully navigate the world of social
media and achieve your business goals.

The Power of Social Media Marketing: How to Build Your Business Presence Online

In the modern age of digital marketing, social media has emerged as a powerful
tool for businesses to build their online presence and connect with their target
audience. With the majority of the world's population actively using social media
platforms, it has become essential for businesses of all sizes to incorporate social
media marketing into their overall marketing strategy.

Social media marketing allows businesses to reach a vast audience, build brand
awareness, and establish a strong online presence. By creating compelling content
and engaging with their audience, businesses can foster meaningful relationships
with their followers and turn them into loyal customers.
To harness the power of social media marketing, it's crucial to define your goals,
identify your target audience, and choose the right social media platforms that
align with your business goals. Once you have established your online identity, it's
important to create a content strategy that is tailored to your audience's
preferences and interests.
Posting regularly and sharing valuable content that resonates with your audience
is key to building you following on social media. It's also essential to interact with
your audience through comments, messages, and live videos, as this can help you
build trust and establish long-lasting relationships.
Social media marketing can also be used to drive traffic to your website, generate
leads, and increase sales. By incorporating call-to-actions and sharing relevant
content that leads back to your website, you can increase the chances of
converting your followers into customers.

To measure the success of your social media marketing efforts, it's essential to
track your metrics and analyze your results. This can help you refine your social
media strategy and optimize your efforts for maximum results.
In conclusion, social media marketing has become a crucial component of
modern-day marketing, and businesses that fail to incorporate it into their overall
strategy risk falling behind. By following these tips and best practices, businesses
can harness the power of social media to build their online presence, connect with
their target audience, and achieve their business goals.

Growing Your Business Through Social Media: Strategies for Success

Social media has become a vital component of real estate marketing, providing
realtors with an unparalleled opportunity to reach and engage with potential
clients. With over three billion people actively using social media, it has become
essential for real estate agents to incorporate social media marketing into their
overall marketing strategy.
One effective strategy for growing your real estate business through social media
is to establish a strong online presence. This involves creating profiles on multiple
social media platforms such as Facebook, Instagram, Twitter, and Linkedin, and
posting high-quality content that showcases your listings, expertise, and
personality.
Another important strategy for success on social media is to focus on building
relationships with your followers. This involves responding to comments and
messages promptly, sharing valuable information about the real estate market,

and engaging with your followers in a meaningful way. By building trust and
establishing relationships with your followers, you can turn them into loyal clients
and advocates for your business.
Social media advertising can also be a powerful tool for growing your real estate
business and reaching new audiences. Platforms like Facebook and Instagram
offer robust advertising capabilities that allow realtors to target specific audiences
based on demographics, interests, and behavior. By using targeted advertising,
real estate agents can reach potential clients with a higher likelihood of converting
into paying customers.
It's also important to use social media to showcase your listings and highlight your
expertise. By using high-quality images and videos, you can provide potential
clients with a virtual tour of your properties and highlight their unique features.
Additionally, by sharing your knowledge and expertise about the real estate market,
you can position yourself as a thought leader in your industry and attract clients
who are looking for a knowledgeable and experienced real estate agent.
Finally, it's crucial to measure the success of your social media efforts through

various metrics and analytics. By tracking your engagement rates, follower growth,
and other key metrics, you can gain valuable insights into what's working and what
needs improvement. This can help you refine your social media strategy over time
and optimize your efforts for maximum results.
In conclusion, social media has become an essential tool for real estate agents
looking to grow their business and reach new clients. By following these strategies
for success, realtors can use social media to establish a strong online presence,
build relationships with their followers, and showcase their expertise and listings
to potential clients.

Maximizing Your Social Media Engagement: A Guide for Entrepreneurs

As an entrepreneur in the real estate industry, social media can be a powerful tool
for engaging with potential clients, building relationships, and growing your

business. However, it's not enough to simply have a social media presence - you
must also focus on maximizing your engagement to make the most of your
efforts.
One of the key strategies for maximizing your social media engagement is to
create content that is tailored to your target audience. This involves understanding
their pain points, interests, and needs, and creating content that speaks directly to
them. By providing valuable information and insights, you can establish yourself as
a thought leader in your industry and build trust with your followers.
Another important strategy for maximizing engagement is to be consistent with
your posting. This means creating a regular schedule for your social media
content and sticking to it. By posting consistently, you can keep your
followers engaged and interested in what you have to say.
It's also crucial to interact with your followers on social media. This involves
responding to comments and messages promptly, thanking followers for their
engagement, and asking for feedback. By engaging with your followers in a
meaningful way, you can build relationships and create a loyal following that is

more likely to convert into paying clients.
Using visuals is another effective way to maximize your social media engagement.
High-quality images and videos can help your content stand out and grab the
attention of your followers. Additionally, using hashtags and tagging relevant
accounts can help you reach a wider audience and increase engagement.
Measuring the success of your social media efforts is also essential for
maximizing engagement. By tracking metrics such as likes, comments, shares,
and follower growth, you can gain valuable insights into what's working and what's
not. This can help you refine your social media strategy over time and optimize
your efforts for maximum engagement and results.
In conclusion, as an entrepreneur in the real estate industry, maximizing your
social media engagement is essential for building relationships, establishing trust,
and growing your business. By creating content that is tailored to your audience,
being consistent with your posting, engaging with your followers, using visuals,
and measuring your success, you can make the most of your social media efforts and achieve success in your industry.

Branding Your Business on Social Media: Creating a Cohesive Online identity

In today's digital age, social media has become an essential tool for businesses to
connect with their target audience and build a strong online presence. For
entrepreneurs in the real estate industry, creating a cohesive online identity
through social media is crucial for establishing your brand and attracting potential
clients.
The first step in branding your business on social media is to define your unique
value proposition. This involves identifying what sets you apart from other real
estate businesses and communicating that message effectively through your
social media channels. By highlighting your strengths and unique selling points,
you can attract clients who resonate with your brand and increase your overall
engagement.

Consistency is also key when it comes to creating a cohesive online identity. This
means maintaining a consistent visual aesthetic across all of your social media
channels, including your profile picture, cover photo, and color scheme. By using
consistent branding elements, you can create a strong visual identity that
reinforces your brand message and helps you stand out from the competition.
In addition to visual consistency, it's also important to use a consistent tone and
voice in your social media content. This involves choosing a brand voice that
reflects your values and personality and using it consistently in your social media
captions, comments, and messages. By developing a consistent brand voice, you
can establish a sense of trust and credibility with your audience and build a strong
relationship with potential clients.
Another key strategy for branding your business on social media is to focus on
providing value to your audience. This involves creating content that is
educational, informative, and engaging, and that speaks directly to the needs and
pain points of your target audience. By providing value through your social media
content, you can establish yourself as a trusted authority in your industry and build

a loyal following of engaged and interested followers. Finally, it's important to measure the success of your branding efforts on social media. This involves tracking metrics such as follower growth, engagement rates, and conversion rates, and using that data to refine your social media strategy over time. By regularly analyzing your social media data and adjusting your approach as needed, you can ensure that your branding efforts are effective and aligned with your overall business goals.

In conclusion, branding your business on social media is a powerful way to establish your online presence and attract potential clients in the real estate industry. By defining your unique value proposition, maintaining visual and tonal consistency, providing value to your audience, and measuring your success, you can create a cohesive online identity that sets you apart from the competition and helps you achieve success in your business.

Harnessing the Influence of Social Media: Building a Community Around Your Brand

Social media has become a powerful tool for entrepreneurs in the real estate
industry to build a community around its brand and establish itself as
industry leaders. By harnessing the influence of social media, real estate
businesses can reach a wider audience, engage with potential clients, and
establish a loyal following of engaged and interested followers.

The first step in harnessing the influence of social media is to identify your target
audience and create content that speaks directly to their needs and interests. This
involves conducting market research to identify your ideal client and
understanding their pain points, challenges, and goals. By creating content that

addresses these issues, you can establish yourself as a trusted resource and build
a community of engaged followers who turn to you for advice and guidance.
In addition to creating valuable content, it's also important to engage with your
followers on social media. This involves responding to comments and messages,
participating in relevant industry conversations, and building relationships with
other influencers in your industry. By engaging with your audience and building a
community around your brand, you can establish yourself as a thought leader in
the real estate industry and attract potential clients who trust and value your
expertise.
Another key strategy for harnessing the influence of social media is to leverage
user-generated content. This involves encouraging your followers to share their
own experiences with your brand and using that content to promote your business.
By featuring user-generated content on your social media channels, you can build
a sense of community and authenticity around your brand, and encourage others
to engage with your business and share their own experiences.
Finally, it's important to track the success of your social media efforts and adjust

your strategy as needed. This involves monitoring metrics such as follower growth,
engagement rates, and conversion rates, and using that data to refine your
approach over time. By regularly analyzing your social media data and making
adjustments as needed, you can ensure that your social media strategy is aligned
with your overall business goals and delivers maximum impact.
In conclusion, harnessing the influence of social media is a powerful way for
entrepreneurs in the real estate industry to build a community around their brand
and establish themselves as industry leaders. By creating valuable content,
engaging with your audience, leveraging user-generated content, and tracking your
success, you can create a strong online presence that attracts potential clients
and helps you achieve success in your business.

Leveraging Social Media Analytics: Measuring the Impact of Your Online Presence

Social media has become an integral part of the real estate industry, with many
entrepreneurs using it as a tool to build their brand, reach a wider audience, and
generate leads. However, in order to truly understand the impact of your social
media presence, it's important to leverage social media analytics.
Social media analytics refers to the process of collecting and analyzing data from
social media platforms to measure the impact of your online presence. By tracking
metrics such as follower growth, engagement rates, and conversion rates, you can
gain valuable insights into how your social media strategy Is performing and make
data-driven decisions to Improve your approach.
One key metric to track is follower growth, which refers to the number of people
who follow your social media accounts over time. This metric can help you

understand the overall reach of your social media presence and the effectiveness
of your marketing efforts. By analyzing follower growth, you can identify trends
and patterns that can help you refine your approach and attract more followers.
Another important metric to track is engagement rates, which refer to the number
of likes, comments, and shares that your social media content receives. This
metric can help you understand how your audience is interacting with your content
and the level of engagement your brand is generating. By analyzing engagement
rates, you can identify the types of content that resonate with your audience and
adjust your strategy accordingly.
Conversion rates are also a key metric to track, as they refer to the number of
people who take a desired action after interacting with your social media content,
such as filling out a lead form or scheduling a consultation. By tracking conversion
rates, you can understand the effectiveness of your social media strategy in
generating leads and driving business growth.
In addition to these metrics, it's also important to analyze demographic data to
understand your audience and tailor your social media strategy to their needs and

interests. This involves tracking data such as age, gender, location, and interests,
and using that information to create targeted content and campaigns.
By leveraging social media analytics, real estate entrepreneurs can gain valuable
insights into the impact of their online presence and make data-driven decisions to
improve their social media strategy. By tracking metrics such as follower growth,
engagement rates, and conversion rates, as well as analyzing demographic data,
entrepreneurs can create a strong and effective social media presence that drives
business growth and helps them achieve success in the real estate industry.

Standing Out on Social Media: Differentiating Your Business in a Crowded Marketplace

In the competitive world of real estate, standing out on social media can be a
challenge. With so many businesses vying for attention on platforms like
Facebook, Instagram, and Twitter, it's important to find ways to differentiate your
brand and capture the attention of potential clients.
One effective strategy for standing out on social media is to establish a clear and
unique brand identity. This involves developing a consistent visual style, tone of
voice, and messaging that sets your brand apart from the competition. By creating
a cohesive and memorable brand identity, you can establish a strong and
recognizable presence on social media that resonates with your target audience.
Another key strategy for standing out on social media is to create high-quality
content that provides value to your audience. This can include informative blog

posts, engaging videos, stunning photos, and interactive social media posts. By
creating content that is useful, informative, or entertaining, you can capture the
attention of potential clients and establish your brand as a trusted source of
information and expertise in the real estate industry.
In addition to creating great content, it's also important to engage with your
audience on social media. This means responding to comments and messages in
a timely and helpful manner and actively seeking out opportunities to connect with
potential clients. By building relationships with your audience on social media, you
can establish trust and credibility, and increase the likelihood that they will choose
to work with you when they are ready to buy or sell a property.
Another effective strategy for standing out on social media is to leverage paid
advertising. Platforms like Facebook and Instagram offer a variety of advertising
options that can help you reach a wider audience and target your ideal clients. By
creating targeted ads that are tailored to the needs and interests of your audience,
you can increase the visibility of your brand and drive more traffic to your website
or landing pages.

Finally, it's important to track your results and adjust your strategy as needed. This
involves regularly analyzing your social media metrics to identify what is working
well, and what could be improved. By making data-driven decisions and adjusting
your strategy based on the results, you can continually improve your social media
presence and stand out in a crowded marketplace.
In summary, standing out on social media in the real estate industry requires a
thoughtful and strategic approach. By establishing a unique brand identity,
creating valuable content, engaging with your audience, leveraging paid
advertising, and tracking your results, you can differentiate your brand and capture
the attention of potential clients in a crowded marketplace.

Engaging with Your Audience on Social Media: Strategies for Building Trust and Loyalty

Engaging with your audience on social media is a crucial component of building
trust and loyalty in the real estate industry. By providing valuable content and
actively participating in online conversations, you can establish a strong
connection with potential clients and position yourself as a trusted expert in your
field.

One effective strategy for engaging with your audience on social media is to create
a content strategy that focuses on providing value to your followers. This can
include informative blog posts, engaging videos, and helpful tips and advice
related to the real estate industry. By creating content that is useful and
informative, you can establish your brand as a valuable resource for potential
clients and build trust and credibility.

Another key strategy for engaging with your audience on social media is to be

responsive and attentive to their needs. This means regularly monitoring your
social media channels and responding to comments, questions, and feedback in a
timely and helpful manner. By showing that you are listening to your audience and
are willing to provide personalized support and assistance, you can build a strong
sense of trust and loyalty.
In addition to being responsive to your audience, it's also important to actively
participate in online conversations and engage with other users on social media.
This can involve sharing and commenting on relevant content, participating in
industry-related discussions, and seeking out opportunities to connect with
potential clients. By engaging with your audience and participating in online
conversations, you can establish yourself as a thought leader in your field and
build a strong reputation for expertise and knowledge.
Another effective strategy for engaging with your audience on social media is to
leverage the power of visual content. Platforms like Instagram and Pinterest offer
a variety of visual content options, including photos, videos, and infographics, that
can help you capture the attention of potential clients and build a strong and

recognizable brand presence. By creating visually compelling content that tells a
story and evokes emotion, you can establish a deeper connection with your
audience and build a sense of trust and loyalty.
Finally, it's important to measure your results and adjust your strategy as needed.
This involves regularly tracking your social media metrics, such as engagement
rates and follower growth, to identify what is working well and what could be
improved. By making data-driven decisions and adjusting your strategy based on
the results, you can continually improve your social media engagement and build
trust and loyalty with your audience.
In summary, engaging with your audience on social media is a critical component
of building trust and loyalty in the real estate industry. By providing valuable
content, being responsive and attentive to your audience's needs, and actively
participating in online conversations, leveraging visual content, and tracking your
results, you can establish a strong and meaningful connection with potential
clients and position yourself as a trusted expert in your field.

Staying Relevant on Social Media: Tips for Maintaining Your Business's Online Presence

In today's digital age, maintaining a strong online presence is crucial for any
business, and the real estate industry is no exception. With the ever-evolving world
of social media, it can be challenging to keep up and stay relevant. However, by
implementing the right strategies, you can ensure that your business remains
visible and top-of-mind for your target audience.
To stay relevant on social media, it's important to start by understanding your

audience and their preferences. This includes identifying the platforms they use

the most and tailoring your content to suit their interests. Consistency is key when

it comes to maintaining a strong online presence, so it's essential to establish a

regular posting schedule that aligns with your audience's engagement patterns.

Another important aspect of staying relevant on social media is keeping up with

industry trends and news. This not only demonstrates your expertise in the field

but also shows that your business is up-to-date with the latest developments.

Sharing relevant and insightful content can help position your business as a

thought leader and keep your audience engaged. Engaging with your audience is also crucial for maintaining your business's online

presence. This involves responding to comments and messages promptly, asking

for feedback and opinions, and actively seeking out conversations with your

followers. By building strong relationships with your audience, you can establish

trust and loyalty, leading to increased engagement and brand advocacy.

Finally, tracking your social media metrics and adjusting your strategies

accordingly is essential for staying relevant and maintaining a strong online presence. By analyzing your data, you can identify what's working and what's not,

allowing you to make informed decisions and improve your social media

performance over time.

In summary, staying relevant on social media requires a strategic approach that

takes into account your audience's preferences, industry trends, engagement

patterns, and metrics. By implementing these strategies consistently, you can

maintain a strong online presence for your real estate business and stay top-of-

mind for your target audience.

CHAPTER FOUR

BUILDING LEADS AND GETTING CLIENTS.

Building leads and getting clients is essential for any business looking to grow and
succeed. In today's fast-paced and highly competitive market, it's important to
have a solid strategy in place to generate and convert leads into paying customers.
The first step in building leads and getting clients is understanding your target
market. This involves identifying the ideal client for your business and tailoring
your marketing efforts to reach them. By understanding your target market's pain
points, needs, and desires, you can create messaging that speaks directly to them
and sets your business apart from the competition.
Once you've identified your target market, building your network is the next step.
Leveraging relationships with colleagues, industry contacts, and even friends and

family can be an effective way to generate leads and referrals. Building a strong
online presence through social media and your website is also crucial in attracting
potential clients.

Offering value to potential clients is another key strategy in building leads and
getting clients. Establishing your expertise and building trust through thought
leadership content, case studies, and testimonials can help potential clients see
the value of your services and increase the likelihood of them becoming paying
customers.

Developing a referral program is another effective way to generate leads and get
clients. Encouraging word-of-mouth marketing through satisfied customers can be
a powerful tool in attracting new business.

Implementing lead generation strategies such as email marketing, targeted
advertising and event marketing can also help maximize your outreach and
conversion rates. It's important to track and analyze your results to measure
the success of your lead generation efforts and make necessary adjustments to your
strategy.

Finally, converting leads into clients requires best practices for closing deals and building relationships. This includes effective communication, active listening, and addressing client concerns and objections in a timely and professional manner.

In conclusion, building leads and getting clients requires a combination of targeted marketing efforts, relationship building, offering value, and implementing effective lead generation strategies. By focusing on these key areas and continually tracking and analyzing your results, you can build a strong client base and achieve long- term success for your business.

Understanding Your Target Market: identifying and Attracting Your Ideal Clients

Understanding your target market is crucial when it comes to building leads and getting clients for your business. You need to identify and attract your ideal clients to increase your chances of success. The first step is to conduct market research and gather data on your potential client's needs, preferences, and behaviors. This

information will help you tailor your marketing strategies to meet their needs and
stand out from the competition.
Once you have a clear understanding of your target market, it's important to create
a strong brand identity that appeals to your ideal clients. This includes developing
a unique value proposition and messaging that resonates with them. Your brand
identity should be consistent across all marketing channels, including social
media, email marketing, and advertising.
In addition to branding, you can attract your ideal clients by offering valuable
content that educates and informs them about your industry or niche. This content
can include blog posts, videos, webinars, and e-books. By providing valuable
information, you can establish yourself as an authority in your field and build trust
with your potential clients.
Networking is another effective strategy for attracting your ideal clients. Attend
industry events, join professional associations, and connect with other
professionals in your field. These connections can lead to referrals and new
business opportunities.
Finally, it's important to have a clear call-to-action (CTA) on all your marketing

materials. This can be a free consultation, a downloadable resource, or an invitation to join your email list. A strong CTA can help convert potential clients into actual clients.

In summary, building leads and getting clients requires a deep understanding of your target market, a strong brand identity, valuable content, networking, and clear CTAs. By implementing these strategies, you can attract and retain your ideal clients and grow your business.

Building Your Network: Leveraging Relationships to Generate Leads

Building a robust network is a crucial element in generating leads and expanding

your client base in the competitive world of real estate. To succeed, you need to
know how to leverage your relationships, both online and offline. This involves
creating a network of connections, including past and current clients, colleagues,
industry professionals, and even family and friends.
To build your network effectively, you must be strategic in your approach. Start by
identifying your target audience and understanding their needs, preferences, and
pain points. Then, seek out relevant networking opportunities, such as industry
conferences, meetups, and online forums. Attend local events, host open houses,
and volunteer for community activities to expand your reach and make new
connections.
Once you have established connections, nurture them with personalized and
consistent communication. Keep your contacts updated on your latest listings,
market trends, and industry insights. Share valuable content that aligns with their
interests and needs, such as home improvement tips, local events, and housing
market updates.
To maximize your network's potential, don't forget to leverage social media
platforms like Linkedin, Facebook, and Twitter. Connect with industry thought

leaders, join relevant groups and participate in discussions. Use these platforms
to showcase your expertise and build credibility with potential clients.

In summary, building a strong network is essential to generating leads and
growing your business in the real estate industry. By identifying your target
the audience, seeking out relevant networking opportunities, and nurturing your
connections, you can establish yourself as a trusted and reliable agent, and attract
your ideal clients.

Creating a Strong Online Presence: Using Social Media and Your Website to Attract Clients

In today's digital age, having a strong online presence is critical for any business,
especially for those in the real estate industry. With the majority of homebuyers
starting their search online, having a well-crafted online presence can be the key to
attracting and retaining clients.
Social media and websites are powerful tools that can help you establish and
maintain your online presence. Social media platforms such as Facebook,
Instagram and Linkedin provide a great opportunity to showcase your properties,
share your expertise, and engage with your followers. By consistently posting high-
quality content that resonates with your target audience, you can establish
yourself as a thought leader and build a loyal following.
Your website is another important component of your online presence. A well-designed website can serve as a virtual storefront, showcasing your properties
and providing valuable information to potential clients. Make sure your website is

user-friendly, easy to navigate, and optimized for search engines. Use high-quality
images and videos to showcase your properties, and make sure your site is
mobile-friendly to reach a wider audience.

Another important aspect of creating a strong online presence is managing your
online reputation. Online reviews and ratings can have a significant impact on your
business, so it's important to actively manage and respond to any reviews you
receive. Use social listening tools to monitor what people are saying about your
business, and take steps to address any negative feedback.

In summary, creating a strong online presence is crucial for attracting clients in the
real estate industry. By leveraging social media, optimizing your website, and
managing your online reputation, you can establish yourself as a trusted expert
and attract new clients to your business.

Offering Value to Potential Clients: Establishing Your Expertise and Build Trust

In the highly competitive world of real estate, standing out from the crowd can be
challenging. One of the most effective ways to establish yourself as a credible and
trustworthy real estate agent is by offering value to potential clients. By
showcasing your expertise, sharing valuable insights, and providing helpful
resources, you can build a loyal following and win the trust of your audience.
One key to offering value is understanding your target market and its unique
needs and challenges. By tailoring your messaging and content to your ideal
clients, you can establish yourself as a go-to resource for all things real estate.

This can include providing tips and advice on everything from home buying and
selling to home renovation and interior design.
In addition to offering valuable content, it's important to establish yourself as an
expert in your field. This can be done by creating and sharing content that
showcases your knowledge and experience, such as blog posts, social media
posts, and video content. By consistently providing informative and helpful
content, you can position yourself as a trusted authority in the real estate industry.
Another key to offering value is building relationships with potential clients. This
can be done through social media engagement, email marketing, and other forms
of communication. By consistently engaging with your audience and providing
personalized attention, you can build trust and establish long-term relationships
with potential clients.
Ultimately, offering value to potential clients is about creating a win-win situation.
By providing helpful resources and establishing yourself as a credible export, you
can attract clients who are seeking your specific expertise and services. In turn,
these clients can help you grow your business and achieve your professional
goals.

Developing a Referral Program: Encouraging Word-of-Mouth Marketing to Generate Leads

In the competitive world of real estate, word-of-mouth marketing can be a powerful
tool for generating leads and building a strong client base. Developing a referral
program can be an effective way to encourage this type of marketing and increase
your chances of success. By creating a program that rewards clients and partners
for referring new business, you can leverage your existing relationships and tap
into the power of personal recommendations. But developing a successful referral
program takes more than just offering a reward - it requires a strategic approach

that focuses on building trust, establishing credibility, and delivering exceptional
service. In this guide, we'll explore the key elements of a successful referral
program in real estate, including how to identify your target audience, create
incentives that motivate action, and track your results. We'll also share best
practices for developing strong relationships with your clients and partners, so you
can foster a culture of referrals and establish yourself as a trusted resource in your
industry. With the right strategy in place, you can harness the power of word-of-
mouth marketing to grow your business and build a loyal client base that will
sustain you for years to come.

Implementing Lead Generation Strategies: Maximizing Your Outreach and Conversion Rates

In the world of real estate, lead generation is the key to success. Without a steady

stream of leads, your business can quickly become stagnant. But with so many
different strategies and channels available, it can be overwhelming to know where
to start. That's why it's important to have a plan in place for implementing lead-generation strategies that maximize your outreach and conversion rates.
From optimizing your website for search engines to leveraging the power of social
media advertising, there are a multitude of tactics you can use to attract potential
clients and convert them into leads. It's also crucial to track your results and make
adjustments as needed to ensure that you're seeing the best possible return on
your investment.
But lead generation is only one piece of the puzzle. It's important to have a solid
plan in place for nurturing and converting those leads into clients. This includes
establishing trust and credibility through content marketing and demonstrating
your expertise through educational resources and personalized communication.
By offering value to your leads and staying top-of-mind, you can increase your
chances of closing the deal and turning those leads into satisfied clients.
Ultimately, the key to successful lead generation in real estate is to stay focused,

remain consistent, and be open to trying new strategies and tactics. With the right
approach, you can build a strong pipeline of leads that will keep your business
growing and thriving for years to come.

Converting Leads into Clients: Best Practices for Closing Deals and Building Relationships

Converting leads into clients is the ultimate goal of any real estate business, but it
can often be a challenging process. To be successful, it's essential to have a solid
strategy in place that prioritizes relationship-building and effective
communication. From the initial contact to the final contract, every step of the
process is an opportunity to strengthen your connection with potential clients and
build trust.

One key aspect of converting leads into clients is understanding their needs and
preferences. By taking the time to listen to their concerns and tailor your approach
to their unique situation, you can demonstrate your expertise and show that you
are committed to providing them with the best possible service.

Another important factor is staying organized and following up consistently. Real
estate transactions can be complex and time-consuming, and it's easy for clients
to become overwhelmed or lose track of important details. By keeping detailed
records and providing regular updates, you can help clients feel more confident
and informed throughout the process.

Ultimately, the key to successfully converting leads into clients is building
relationships based on trust and mutual respect. By demonstrating your value and
expertise, staying organized and communicative, and prioritizing the needs of your
clients, you can establish yourself as a trusted advisor and build a loyal client base
that will help you grow your business over time.

Tracking and Analyzing Your Results: Measuring the Success of Your Lead Generation Efforts.

Lead generation is a crucial aspect of any business, and real estate is no
exception. However, it's not enough to simply generate leads; you need to track
and analyze your results to ensure that your efforts are effective and efficient. By
doing so, you can identify areas that need improvement, refine your strategies, and
ultimately, increase your ROI. This is where tracking and analyzing your results
come into play. In this topic, we'll explore the importance of tracking and analyzing
your lead generation efforts, the tools and metrics available to measure your
success, and how to use this data to make informed decisions that will help you
grow your business in real estate. We'll delve into the key performance indicators
(KPIs) that matter most in lead generation, such as conversion rates, lead quality,

and cost per lead, and explain how to use them to optimize your lead generation
strategy. By the end of this topic, you'll have a clear understanding of how to track
and analyze your results, and how to use this information to continually improve
your lead generation efforts in real estate.

CHAPTER FIVE

THE OPEN HOUSE.

The Open House is a key event in the world of real estate, offering potential buyers
a chance to explore properties and connect with real estate professionals. In the
fast-paced and constantly evolving world of real estate, the Open House is tried-
and-true methods for showcasing properties and bringing buyers and sellers
together. It's an opportunity for prospective buyers to experience the space,
interact with agents, and make informed decisions about their future.
Welcome to the Open House, where the possibilities are endless. This event offers
buyers the chance to explore their dream homes and see the features and amenities in
person, and connect with real estate agents who can provide expert guidance and
personalized attention. From the moment you walk through the door, you'll feel the
warmth and comfort of the space, envisioning yourself living your best life in your
new home.
The Open House is the perfect place to discover the best deals in real estate, with

exclusive offers and promotions only available at these events. It's a chance to

explore a wide range of properties, from cozy bungalows to luxurious retreats, and

find the perfect space to suit your lifestyle and budget. Whether you're a first-time

homebuyer or a seasoned investor, the Open House offers something for

everyone.

Step inside your future home and experience the feeling of belonging that comes

with finding the perfect space for you and your loved ones. Get a sneak peek of our

properties and discover the fine details that make each one a true masterpiece,

from the quality of materials used to the innovative technology integrated

throughout. This is your chance to explore every nook and cranny of the properties

on display, taking in the stunning views, luxurious amenities, and expert

craftsmanship that make each home truly unique.

Join us for a tour of our Open House and let our knowledgeable professionals

guide you through the process of finding your dream home. With expert guidance

and personalized attention, you can explore the finer details of each property,

learning about the architectural design, the quality of materials used, and the

cutting-edge technology integrated throughout. At the Open House, you can make
informed decisions about your future, connecting with real estate professionals
who can help you navigate the complex world of real estate.
Your perfect home is waiting for you, just waiting to be discovered. Take a look
around and let the feeling of coming home wash over you, as you imagine yourself

building a life in a space that is truly yours. The Open House is more than just an
event - it's a gateway to a new chapter in your life, where you can create memories,
build relationships, and grow as a person. Don't miss your chance to see our
properties in person, and take the first step towards a brighter future filled with
endless possibilities. The Open House is calling, Are you ready to answer?

1. Welcome to the Open House, where the possibilities are endless, and the
opportunities are abundant.
2. Explore Your Dream Home Today and see firsthand what it feels like to live in a
space that's tailored to your needs and desires.
3. Discover the Best Deals in Real Estate and find your perfect home without

breaking the bank. Our real estate professionals are here to guide you every
step of the way.

4. Step Inside Your Future Home and experience the unique features and
amenities that make each property stand out.

5. Get a Sneak Peek of Our Properties and envision yourself living your best life in
a space that's designed to meet your every need.

6. Join Us for a Tour of Our Open House and get a behind-the-scenes look at the
properties that could become your next home.

7. Your Perfect Home is Waiting for You, and we're here to help you find it. From
cozy bungalows to spacious family homes, we have something for everyone.

8. Take a Look Around - Your Dream Home Awaits, and we invite you to explore
every corner of our properties, from the basement to the rooftop terrace.

9. Meet Your New Home at the Open House, where you can connect with other
buyers, network with real estate professionals, and make your dreams a reality.

10. Don't Miss Your Chance to See Our Properties in Person - book your tour today
and discover why our Open House events are the talk of the town.

Use this catchphrase or should I say techniques and you will be much more surprised at how successful you will become.

CHAPTER SIX

LISTING PRESENTATION

Introducing Your Dream Home to the Market

Introducing your dream home to the market is an exciting and crucial step in the
real estate process. It's a chance to showcase the unique features and amenities

of your property and connect with potential buyers who are searching for their
perfect home. A successful market introduction requires careful planning,
strategic marketing, and expert guidance from experienced real estate
professionals who understand the nuances of the industry.
At our agency, we specialize in introducing your dream home to the market in a
way that maximizes exposure, generates interest, and ultimately leads to a
successful sale. We begin by conducting a thorough analysis of your property,
taking into account its unique features, location, and potential buyer
demographics. From there, we create a comprehensive marketing strategy that
leverages the latest tools and technologies to reach the widest possible audience.
Our team of real estate experts has a deep understanding of the local market,
including pricing trends, buyer preferences, and market conditions. We work
closely with you to develop a pricing strategy that reflects the true value of your
property and attracts the right buyers. By leveraging our industry knowledge and
experience, we ensure that your property is positioned for success from the very
beginning.

We understand that presentation is key when it comes to introducing your dream
home to the market. That's why we offer professional staging and photography
services, which help to highlight the best features of your property and create a
warm and inviting atmosphere. Our team works with you to ensure that your
property is presented in the best possible light, both in person and online.
We believe that communication and transparency are essential to a successful
market introduction. Throughout the process, we keep you informed of all
developments, providing regular updates and feedback from potential buyers. We
also work to ensure that you are comfortable with the entire process, answering
any questions or concerns you may have along the way.
At our agency, we are committed to being your trusted partner in introducing your
dream home to the market. We work tirelessly to bring your property to its full
potential, leveraging our expertise, market knowledge, and innovative marketing
strategies to achieve a successful sale. So, if you're ready to introduce your dream
home to the market, we're here to help you every step of the way.

A Comprehensive Guide to Selling Your Property

Selling your property can be a complex and challenging process, requiring a great
deal of knowledge and experience to navigate successfully. From understanding
market trends and pricing strategies to negotiating contracts and closing the deal,
there are many important factors to consider when selling your real estate.
To help guide you through this process, we have created a comprehensive guide
that will provide you with all the information you need to sell your property
effectively. We'll start by exploring the current state of the real estate market
and examining key trends and factors that can impact the sale of your property.
Next, we'll delve into the preparation process, offering insights on how to get your
property in top shape for listing and showings. This will include tips on staging
your home, making repairs and upgrades, and determining an appropriate asking
price.

Once your property is ready to go to market, we'll provide guidance on the most
effective ways to advertise and promote your listing, from creating eye-catching
photos and videos to use social media and online listing platforms to reach
potential buyers.

As you start to receive offers and negotiate with potential buyers, we'll provide tips
and strategies for navigating this complex process, including how to evaluate
offers, understand contingencies and handle any issues that may arise during the
inspection or appraisal process.

Finally, will offer guidance on closing the deal, from finalizing the contract and
arranging the transfer of ownership to navigating the legal and financial aspects of
the transaction.

Whether you're a seasoned real estate investor or a first-time seller, our
comprehensive guide to selling your property will equip you with the knowledge
and resources you need to make informed decisions, maximize your return on
investment, and achieve a successful sale.

Why Choose Us for Your Listing Presentation

If you're looking to sell your property in today's competitive real estate market, it's
important to partner with a trusted and experienced team that can help you
achieve your goals. At our real estate agency, we understand the complexities of
the selling process, and we're committed to providing our clients with the highest
level of service and expertise.
When you choose us for your listing presentation, you can expect a comprehensive
and personalized approach that is tailored to your unique needs and goals. We'll
start by conducting a thorough analysis of your property, taking into account key
factors such as location, size, and condition to determine the most effective
pricing strategy.
Next, we'll work with you to develop a customized marketing plan that leverages
the latest tools and technologies to attract potential buyers and generate interest
in your property. From the professional photography and virtual tours to targeted

advertising and social media campaigns, we'll use a range of strategies to ensure
that your listing receives maximum exposure and generates the highest possible
offers.
Throughout the selling process, our team will be there to provide guidance and
support, answering your questions, and addressing any concerns you may have.
Whether you're negotiating offers, navigating contingencies, or finalizing the sale,
we'll be with you every step of the way, leveraging our deep industry knowledge
and experience to help you achieve a successful outcome.
So why choose us for your listing presentation? Simply put, we offer the expertise,
resources, and dedication you need to achieve your real estate goals. With our
team on your side, you can rest assured that you'll receive the highest level of
service and support, and that we'll work tirelessly to help you achieve a successful
sale.

Understanding the Real Estate Market and Pricing Strategies

Understanding the real estate market and pricing strategies is critical for anyone
looking to buy or sell a property. In today's dynamic and competitive market, pricing
your property correctly can mean the difference between a successful sale and a
listing that languishes on the market for months.
At the heart of pricing strategy is a deep understanding of the real estate market,
including current trends, supply and demand dynamics, and local economic
conditions. By staying up to date on the latest market data and trends, our team is
able to provide our clients with expert guidance and insights that help them make
informed decisions about pricing and positioning their property.
When it comes to pricing strategy, there are many different factors to consider.

These may include the property's location, condition, size, and amenities, as well
as the local real estate market and competition from other listings in the area. Our
team takes a holistic approach to pricing, considering all of these factors and
more to arrive at a pricing strategy that is tailored to your unique needs and goals.
One key tool in our pricing toolkit is comparative market analysis (CMA), which
involves analyzing recent sales of comparable properties in the area to determine
a fair market value for your property. This data-driven approach helps us ensure
that your property is priced correctly and positioned to attract potential buyers.
Another important consideration in pricing strategy is the role of negotiation. Our
team has extensive experience in negotiating with potential buyers, and we use
this expertise to help you achieve the highest possible price for your property.
Whether you're dealing with multiple offers or navigating contingencies and other
issues, we'll be there to guide you every step of the way.
In short, understanding the real estate market and pricing strategies is critical for
anyone looking to buy or sell a property. By partnering with our team, you'll benefit
from our deep industry expertise and data-driven approach to pricing, ensuring

that you receive the highest possible return on your real estate investment.

Marketing Your Property to Maximize Exposure

Marketing your property to maximize exposure is a critical component of any
successful real estate sale. In today's competitive market, it's not enough to simply
list your property and hopes for the best. Instead, you need a comprehensive and
strategic marketing plan that leverages the latest tools and technologies to attract
potential buyers and generate interest in your property. At our real estate agency, we specialize in creating customized marketing plans
that are tailored to the unique needs and goals of our clients. Whether you're
selling a high-end luxury property or a modest family home, we'll work with you to
develop a plan that is designed to maximize exposure and generate the highest
possible offers.
One key component of our marketing strategy is professional photography and

videography. We believe that high-quality visuals are critical to capturing the attention of potential buyers, and we use the latest equipment and techniques to create stunning images and videos that showcase your property in the best possible light.

In addition to photography and videography, we also leverage a range of digital marketing tools and platforms to promote your listing to a wide audience of potential buyers. This may include targeted social media advertising, email marketing campaigns, and online listing platforms that are specifically designed to attract real estate buyers.

Of course, marketing is not just about digital tools and technology. We also believe in the power of personal connections and relationships to generate interest in your property. That's why we work closely with our network of real estate agents and industry professionals to promote your listing and connect with potential buyers who may be interested in your property?

Ultimately, our goal is to create a marketing plan that is tailored to your unique needs and goals and that is designed to generate maximum exposure and interest in your property. By partnering with our team, you'll benefit from our deep industry

expertise and our commitment to providing you with the highest level of service
and support.

Negotiation Strategies for a Successful Sale

Negotiation strategies are a critical component of any successful real estate sale.
Whether you're a buyer or a seller, negotiating the terms of a sale can be a
complex and challenging process. That's why it's important to work with a real
estate agent who has extensive experience in negotiating successful deals, and
who can help you navigate the negotiation process with confidence and skill.
At our real estate agency, we have a team of skilled and experienced negotiators
who specialize in helping our clients achieve their real estate goals. We use a
variety of proven negotiation strategies and tactics to help our clients secure the
best possible deals, while also ensuring that their interests are protected
throughout the process.

One key negotiation strategy that we employ is preparation. Before entering into
negotiations, we take the time to research the market and gather all of the relevant
data and information that will be needed to make informed decisions. This
includes analyzing comparable sales data, understanding local market trends and
conditions, and identifying potential obstacles or challenges that may need to be
addressed during negotiations.

Another important negotiation strategy is effective communication. We believe
that clear and open communication is essential to successful negotiations, and
we work closely with our clients to understand their goals and priorities and to
communicate their needs and interests to potential buyers or sellers.

We also believe in the power of leverage when it comes to negotiating successful
real estate deals. This may involve identifying and highlighting unique features or
benefits of your property, or leveraging competing offers to negotiate the best
possible deal for our clients.

Of course, negotiation is not just about getting the best possible price for your
property. It's also about ensuring that the terms of the sale are fair and equitable

and that your interests are protected throughout the process. That's why we
always take a holistic approach to negotiations, considering all of the factors that
are important to our clients and working to achieve a successful outcome that
meets their needs and priorities.
In short, negotiation strategies are a critical component of any successful real
estate sale. By working with our team of skilled negotiators, you'll benefit from our
extensive experience and expertise in navigating complex negotiations and our
commitment to helping you achieve your real estate goals.

Professional Staging and Photography Services

Professional staging and photography services are essential when it comes to
marketing and selling your property in today's competitive real estate market. At
our real estate agency, we understand the power of high-quality visuals and
expertly staged homes, and we offer a range of professional services designed to

help our clients showcase their properties in the best possible light.

One key component of our professional services is our expert staging team. We work with a team of experienced staging professionals who have a keen eye for design and a deep understanding of what it takes to make a property look its best.

They'll work with you to create a customized staging plan that highlights your property's unique features and creates a warm, inviting atmosphere that will appeal to potential buyers.

In addition to staging, we also offer professional photography and videography services that are designed to showcase your property in the best possible light.

We believe that high-quality visuals are critical to attracting potential buyers and generating interest in your property, and we use the latest equipment and techniques to capture stunning images and videos that showcase your property's unique features and benefits.

Our team of photographers and videographers is skilled at capturing the essence of your property, highlighting its unique features, and showcasing its most attractive qualities. From wide-angle shots that capture the full scope of your

property, to close-up shots that showcase intricate details and finishes, we use a
range of techniques to create images and videos that are sure to impress potential
buyers and generate interest in your property.
Of course, professional staging and photography are not just about creating a
beautiful visual experience. They are also essential when it comes to marketing
and selling your property. That's why we leverage a range of digital marketing tools
and platforms to promote your listing to a wide audience of potential buyers. From
targeted social media advertising to email marketing campaigns and online listing
platforms, we use a variety of techniques to ensure that your property receives
maximum exposure and generates the highest possible offers.
In short, professional staging and photography services are a critical component
of any successful real estate sale. By working with our team of experts, you'll
benefit from our deep industry expertise, our commitment to providing you with
the highest level of service and support, and our proven track record of success in
helping our clients achieve their real estate goals.

Communication and Transparency Throughout the Process

At our real estate agency, we believe that clear communication and transparency
throughout the process are essential to a successful real estate transaction.
Buying or selling a property can be a complex and sometimes stressful process,
but we believe that keeping our clients informed and engaged every step of the
way can help alleviate some of that stress and ensure that everyone is on the
same page.

From the very beginning of the process, we make it a priority to establish clear
lines of communication with our clients. We take the time to listen to their needs
and priorities, and we work closely with them to develop a customized plan that
aligns with their goals and helps them achieve the best possible outcome.

Throughout the process, we keep our clients informed of all important
developments and provide regular updates on the status of their transactions.

Whether it's providing feedback from potential buyers, sharing market data and
insights, or updating them on the progress of negotiations, we believe that keeping
our clients informed and engaged is critical to their satisfaction and success.

In addition to clear communication, we also prioritize transparency in all of our
dealings. We believe that our clients have the right to know what's going on at all
times, and we make it a point to be open and honest about all aspects of the
transaction, from pricing and negotiations to potential issues or challenges that
may arise.
By prioritizing communication and transparency throughout the process, we help
our clients feel more confident and empowered in their decision-making, and we
ensure that they have all of the information they need to make informed choices
that align with their goals and priorities. Whether you're buying or selling a
property, you can trust us to keep you informed, engaged, and confident at every step
of the way.
In short, clear communication and transparency are essential to a successful real
estate transaction. At our real estate agency, we prioritize these values in all of our
dealings, and we are committed to keeping our clients informed and engaged
throughout the process. By working with us, you'll benefit from our deep industry
expertise, our commitment to providing the highest level of service and support,

and our unwavering dedication to helping you achieve your real estate goals.

Your Trusted Partner in Selling Your Property
When it comes to selling your property in the competitive real estate market,
having a trusted partner by your side can make all the difference. At our real estate
agency, we are committed to being that trusted partner for our clients, providing
them with the guidance, support, and expertise they need to achieve their goals
and get the best possible outcome.
We understand that selling a property can be complex and sometimes
overwhelming process, which is why we work closely with our clients every step of
the way to ensure a smooth and successful transaction. From developing a
customized marketing plan that maximizes exposure and generates interest in
your property, to negotiate the best possible deal and manage all of the details
of the transaction, we are there for you every step of the way.
One of the key advantages of working with us is our deep industry expertise and

experience. Our team of real estate professionals has a wealth of knowledge and
insights into the local market, as well as the latest industry trends and best
practices. We use this expertise to help our clients make informed decisions and
navigate the sometimes complex and confusing world of real estate sales.

But it's not just our expertise that sets us apart. We are also committed to
providing our clients with the highest level of service and support, from our
responsive and knowledgeable customer service team to our skilled and
experienced agents who are dedicated to achieving the best possible outcome for
our clients.

We know that selling a property is a big decision, and we take that responsibility
seriously. That's why we are committed to being a true partner to our clients,
providing them with the guidance, support, and expertise they need to make
informed decisions and achieve their goals. Whether you're selling a property for
the first time or the fifth, you can trust us to be there for you every step of the way.

In short, when it comes to selling your property in the real estate market, you need
a trusted partner by your side. At our real estate agency, we are that partner,

providing you with the expertise, support, and
commitment you need to achieve
the best possible outcome. Contact us today to learn
more about how we can help
you sell your property with confidence and success.

Bringing Your Property to Its Full Potential through Our Listing Presentation.

At our real estate agency, we believe that every property
has the potential to shine,
and that's why we are committed to bringing out the best
in every listing through
our powerful and effective listing presentation. With our
extensive industry
expertise, our deep understanding of the local market,
and our commitment to

excellence, we work tirelessly to ensure that every property we represent is
showcased in the best possible light.
Our listing presentation is more than just a marketing tool - it's a comprehensive
strategy that combines cutting-edge marketing techniques with tried-and-true real
estate practices to generate maximum exposure and interest in your property.
From professional photography and staging services to strategic pricing and
marketing, we leave no stone unturned in our efforts to bring your property to its
full potential.
One of the key advantages of working with us is our personalized approach to
listing presentations. We understand that every property is unique, with its own set
of features, challenges, and selling points, and that's why we take the time to get to
know your property inside and out. We work closely with you to develop a
customized marketing plan that highlights the best aspects of your property and
positions it for success in the competitive real estate market.
But our listing presentation is more than just a marketing plan - it's a commitment
to excellence and dedication to achieving the best possible outcome for our

clients. We are constantly monitoring market trends and adjusting our strategies
to ensure that your property is always positioned for success, and we are always
available to answer your questions and address your concerns throughout the
process.
In short, when it comes to bringing your property to its full potential, you need a
real estate agency that is committed to excellence and dedicated to achieving the
best possible outcome for you. At our real estate agency, we are that partner,
providing you with the personalized attention, industry expertise, and marketing
savvy you need to succeed. Contact us today to learn more about our powerful
and effective listing presentation and how we can help you bring your property to
the next level.

CHAPTER SEVEN

FOLLOW-UP

The Importance of Follow-Up: Enhancing Productivity and Building Relationships.

In the fast-paced world of real estate, the importance of follow-up cannot be
overstated. Effective follow-up not only enhances productivity but also builds
strong and lasting relationships with clients, colleagues, and partners. In an
industry where success is often determined by the ability to close deals, a well-
crafted follow-up strategy can make all the difference. Real estate professionals who prioritize follow-up demonstrate their commitment

to their clients and create a reputation for reliability and dependability. A timely and
personalized follow-up can turn a potential client into a loyal one and can result in
referrals and repeat business. It is not enough to simply make a good first
impression; follow-up is essential for building trust and establishing long-term
relationships.
In the fast-moving world of real estate, deals can fall through, clients can change
their minds, and opportunities can be missed. However, a proactive and consistent
follow-up strategy can help mitigate these risks and keep deals moving forward.
Whether it is a phone call, email, or personal visit, a well-timed follow-up can
ensure that no opportunity is missed and that clients feel supported throughout
the buying or selling process.
In addition to enhancing productivity and building relationships, follow-up can also
provide valuable feedback and insights. By keeping in touch with clients after a
deal has closed, real estate professionals can gain valuable feedback on their
services and identify areas for improvement. This feedback can be used to refine
their approach and improve their overall performance.
In conclusion, the importance of follow-up cannot be overstated in the real estate

industry. A well-crafted follow-up strategy can enhance productivity, build strong
and lasting relationships, mitigate risks, provide valuable feedback, and ultimately
drive success. By prioritizing follow-up, real estate professionals can establish
themselves as reliable partners for their clients and colleagues.

Maximizing Results with Effective Follow-Up Strategies

Maximizing results in the real estate industry requires more than just making initial
connections; it requires implementing effective follow-up strategies that keep
clients engaged and motivated throughout the buying or selling process. By
prioritizing follow-up, real estate professionals can create a lasting impression on
their clients, build trust and increase the likelihood of success.

Effective follow-up strategies can take many forms,
including regular phone calls,
personalized emails, or in-person meetings. By
maintaining consistent
communication with clients, real estate professionals
can stay on top of their minds,
answer questions, and provide valuable insights that
demonstrate their expertise
and commitment.
One of the most effective follow-up strategies is to
provide clients with relevant
and timely information that is tailored to their specific
needs. This could include
market updates, property listings, or insights into the
buying or selling process. By
providing this information in a personalized and
thoughtful way, real estate
professionals can demonstrate their value and establish
themselves as trusted
advisors.
Another key aspect of effective follow-up strategies is to
be responsive and
proactive. Real estate professionals who respond
quickly to client inquiries and
Follow-up promptly on leads and opportunities are more
likely to close deals and
build strong relationships. This requires not only a
commitment to staying
organized and managing time effectively but also a
willingness to go above and
beyond to meet clients' needs.

In addition to enhancing productivity and building relationships, effective follow-up
strategies can also provide valuable insights that can be used to refine and
improve the real estate professional's approach. By tracking and analyzing the
the success of different follow-up strategies, real estate professionals can identify
what works and what doesn't and adjust their approach accordingly.
In conclusion, maximizing results in the real estate industry requires implementing
effective follow-up strategies that keep clients engaged and motivated throughout
the buying or selling process. By prioritizing personalized communication,
responsiveness, and a commitment to providing value, real estate professionals
can establish themselves as trusted advisors and drive success for their clients
and their business.

Don't Let Opportunities Slip Away: Mastering the Art of Follow-Up

In the fast-paced world of real estate, opportunities can slip away in an instant.
Whether it's a potential buyer who is still considering their options or a seller who
is hesitant to commit, effective follow-up can make all the difference in closing
deals and achieving success.
To master the art of follow-up in real estate, it is essential to be proactive,
persistent, and personalized. This means taking the time to understand each
client's unique needs and preferences and tailoring follow-up efforts accordingly. A
thoughtful and timely follow-up can demonstrate a real estate professional's
commitment to their clients and can differentiate them from competitors.
One effective strategy for mastering the art of follow-up is to establish a regular
cadence of communication with clients. This could include regular phone calls,

emails, or in-person meetings, depending on the client's preferences. By
maintaining consistent communication, real estate professionals can stay top of
mind and demonstrate their value as trusted advisors.
Another key aspect of mastering the art of follow-up is to be responsive and timely
in all communications. Real estate professionals who respond quickly to inquiries
and follow up promptly on leads and opportunities are more likely to close deals
and build strong relationships. This requires a commitment to staying organized
and managing time effectively, as well as a willingness to go above and beyond to
meet clients' needs.
In addition to being proactive and responsive, mastering the art of follow-up also
requires a willingness to adapt and adjust strategies as needed. This means
tracking and analyzing the success of different follow-up approaches and
adjusting tactics accordingly. By staying flexible and willing to try new things, real
estate professionals can stay ahead of the competition and capitalize on new
opportunities.
In conclusion, mastering the art of follow-up is essential for success in the real
estate industry. By prioritizing personalized communication, responsiveness, and

willingness to adapt, real estate professionals, can differentiate themselves from
competitors and close more deals. With a thoughtful and persistent follow-up
strategy, opportunities will no longer slip away, but rather turn into successful
transactions and happy clients.

The Power of Persistence: Why Follow-Up is Essential for Success

In the competitive world of real estate, persistence is key to achieving success.
While making initial connections with clients is important, it is often the follow-up
that sets successful real estate professionals apart. Effective follow-up requires a
persistent and proactive approach that demonstrates a commitment to clients and
builds trust over time.
One of the primary reasons why follow-up is essential for success in real estate is
that it helps to build relationships. By maintaining consistent communication with

clients, real estate professionals can stay top of mind and establish themselves as
trusted advisors. This requires more than just sending occasional emails or
making phone calls; it requires a thoughtful and personalized approach that
demonstrates a real understanding of each client's unique needs and preferences.
Another important aspect of the power of persistence in follow-up is that it can
help real estate professionals to overcome objections and close deals. In many
cases, clients may have reservations or concerns that prevent them from
committing to a transaction. By persistently addressing these concerns and
providing solutions, real estate professionals can build trust and confidence,
ultimately leading to successful transactions.
The power of persistence in follow-up can also help real estate professionals to
capitalize on opportunities that might otherwise be missed. By staying alert and
responsive to leads and opportunities, real estate professionals can position
themselves to make the most of every chance to connect with clients and close
deals.
Ultimately, the power of persistence in follow-up comes down to a commitment to

providing value and building trust over time. This requires a persistent and
proactive approach that demonstrates a genuine interest in helping clients achieve
their goals. By focusing on building relationships and providing thoughtful and
personalized communication, real estate professionals can establish themselves
as trusted advisors and drive success for their clients and their business.

In conclusion, the power of persistence in follow-up is essential for success in real
estate. By prioritizing personalized communication, responsiveness, and a
commitment to providing value, real estate professionals can establish
themselves as trusted advisors and drive success for their clients and their
business. With a persistent and proactive follow-up strategy, real estate
professionals can overcome objections, capitalize on opportunities, and ultimately
close more deals.

Beyond the Initial Contact: How to Keep the Momentum Going with Follow-Up

In the world of real estate, the initial contact with a client is just the beginning of a
journey toward a successful transaction. To keep the momentum going
and build toward a successful outcome, effective follow-up is essential. This
requires a strategic and persistent approach that maintains engagement and
communication with clients over time.
One key aspect of effective follow-up in real estate is to stay organized and
focused on key priorities. This means tracking leads, appointments, and follow-up
tasks in a centralized system that enables real estate professionals to stay on top
of their workflow and prioritize their time. With the right tools and systems in
place, real estate professionals can maintain consistent communication with
clients and move transactions forward in a timely and effective manner.
Another important element of effective follow-up is to tailor communications to
each client. This means taking the time to understand their unique
needs and preferences and crafting personalized messages that demonstrate a
real understanding of their situation. By showing clients that they are valued and
understood, real estate professionals can build trust and establish strong

relationships that lead to successful transactions.

In addition to personalized communication, effective follow-up in real estate requires a willingness to go above and beyond to provide value to clients. This might include offering helpful resources or advice, providing referrals to other professionals in the industry, or simply being available to answer questions and address concerns. By demonstrating a commitment to their client's success, real estate professionals can establish themselves as trusted advisors and drive success for their businesses.

Ultimately, effective follow-up in real estate is about more than just maintaining communication; it is about keeping the momentum going and building toward a successful outcome. This requires a strategic and persistent approach that prioritizes organization, personalized communication, and a willingness to provide value. With these elements in place, real estate professionals can differentiate themselves from competitors and drive success for their clients and their business.

In conclusion, beyond the initial contact, effective follow-up is essential for success in real estate. By staying organized, tailoring communication, and

providing value to clients, real estate professionals can keep the momentum going
and build toward successful transactions. With a strategic and persistent follow-
up strategy, real estate professionals can establish themselves as trusted advisors
and drive success for their businesses.

Follow-Up Dos and Don'ts: Tips for Making a Lasting Impression

Effective follow-up is an essential component of success in real estate, but it can
be a delicate balance between being persistent and being pushy. To make a lasting
impression on clients, real estate professionals must navigate the do's and don'ts
of follow-up strategies.
One important "do" of follow-up in real estate is to stay consistent in
communication. This means keeping in touch with clients through a variety of
channels, including email, phone, and social media. By maintaining regular

communication, real estate professionals can stay top of mind and demonstrate
their commitment to helping clients achieve their goals.
Another important "do' of follow-up is to be personal and authentic in
communication. This means taking the time to understand each client's unique
needs and preferences and crafting messages that are tailored to their situation.
By showing clients that they are valued and understood, real estate professionals
can build trust and establish strong relationships that lead to successful
transactions.
On the other hand, there are also several "'don'ts" to keep in mind when it comes to
follow-up in real estate. One common mistake is to be too pushy or aggressive in
communication. This can make clients feel uncomfortable or pressured, and may
ultimately harm the relationship. Instead, real estate professionals should focus on
being helpful and informative, providing resources and guidance that can help
clients make informed decisions.
Another "don't" to keep in mind is to bo disorganized or unresponsive in
communication. This can give clients the impression that they are not a priority, or
that the real estate professional is not taking their needs seriously. To avoid this,

real estate professionals should prioritize organization
and responsiveness,
tracking leads and follow-up tasks in a centralized
system and responding
promptly to client inquiries.
Ultimately, the key to effective follow-up in real estate is
to strike a balance
between persistence and authenticity. By staying
consistent in communication,
being personal and authentic in messaging, and
avoiding pushy or disorganized
communication, real estate professionals can make a
lasting impression on
clients and drive success for their business.
In conclusion, follow-up dos and don'ts are critical for
making a lasting impression
in real estate. By staying consistent, being personal and
authentic, and avoiding
pushy or disorganized communication, real estate
professionals can build trust,
establish strong relationships, and drive success for
their businesses. With a
thoughtful and strategic follow-up strategy, real estate
professionals can
differentiate themselves from competitors and make a
lasting impression on
clients.

From Follow-Up to Follow-Through: Turning Connections into Collaborations

Follow-up is essential for building relationships in real estate, but it's not enough to
simply stay in touch with clients. To truly drive success and establish long-term
collaborations, real estate professionals must also focus on follow-through,
delivering on their promises, and demonstrating their value as trusted partners.
Effective follow-through begins with a deep understanding of each client's needs
and goals. By listening carefully and asking thoughtful questions, real estate
professionals can gain insights into what each client is looking for and what
challenges they may be facing. Armed with this information, real estate
professionals can then develop tailored solutions that meet each client's specific
needs and help them achieve their goals.

Another important element of follow-through in real estate is staying organized
and proactive. This means tracking tasks and follow-up items in a centralized
system, and proactively reaching out to clients to provide updates and progress
reports. By staying on top of tasks and communicating regularly, real estate
professionals can build trust and demonstrate their commitment to helping clients
achieve success.
Perhaps the most critical element of follow-thrOugh in real estate is delivering on
promises. Whether it's providing timely updates, offering valuable resources, or
connecting clients with key stakeholders, real estate professionals must
consistently deliver on their commitments to build trust and establish themselves
as reliable partner. This means setting realistic expectations, communicating
clearly and honestly, and following through on commitments, even if it requires
extra effort or resources.
Ultimately, the key to turning connections into collaborations in real estate is to
focus on follow-through as well as follow-up. By deeply understanding each
client's needs and goals, staying organized and proactive, and consistently

delivering on commitments, real estate professionals can establish themselves as
trusted partners and drive success for their business.
In conclusion, from the follow-up to follow-through, turning connections into
collaborations requires a strategic and thoughtful approach to relationship-
building in real estate. By focusing on understanding each client's unique needs
and goals, staying organized and proactive, and delivering on commitments, real
estate professionals can establish themselves as trusted partners and drive
success for their businesses. With a commitment to follow-through as well as
the follow-up, real estate professionals can differentiate themselves from competitors
and build long-lasting collaborations with clients.

Maximizing Results with Effective Follow-Up Strategies Follow-Up Formula: A Proven Method for Closing Deals and Building Trust

Effective follow-up is an essential ingredient for success in the real estate industry.

By nurturing relationships, building trust, and consistently providing value, real

estate professionals can maximize results and close more deals. But with so

many tasks to manage and leads to follow up on, it can be challenging to develop

a follow-up strategy that works.

That's where the Follow-Up Formula comes in. This proven method for closing

deals and building trust is a powerful tool for real estate professionals looking to

streamline their follow-up process and drive results.

At its core, the Follow-Up Formula is a three-step process that begins with

segmentation. By categorizing leads and contacts based on their needs and

interests, real estate professionals can tailor their follow-up efforts to provide
relevant and valuable information that meets their needs. This not only increases
the chances of conversion but also helps to build trust and rapport with clients.
The second step of the Follow-Up Formula is engagement. This involves reaching
out to leads and contacts in a way that encourages interaction and feedback. By
providing multiple touchpoints and opportunities for engagement, real estate
professionals can demonstrate their value and establish themselves as trusted
resource.
The final step of the Follow-Up Formula is conversion. This involves closing the
deal and delivering on promises made throughout the follow-up process. By
continuing to provide value and staying in touch after the deal has closed, real
estate professionals can build long-term relationships that lead to repeat business
and referrals.
But the Follow-Up Formula isn't just a set-it-and-forget-it approach to follow-up.
Real estate professionals must also contInuously evaluate and optimize their
follow-up efforts to ensure they are delivering maximum results. This involves

tracking metrics, analyzing data, and making adjustments based on feedback and results.

Overall, the Follow-Up Formula is a powerful tool for real estate professionals looking to maximize results with effective follow-up strategies. By segmenting leads, engaging with clients, and converting opportunities into deals, real estate professionals can build trust, establish themselves as experts in their field, and drive success for their business. With a commitment to the Follow-Up Formula and a dedication to continuous improvement, real estate professionals can differentiate themselves from competitors and build long-lasting relationships with clients.

Follow-Up Made Simple: Streamlining Your Process for Better Results

Effective follow-up is critical for real estate professionals looking to build lasting
relationships with clients and close more deals. However, with so many leads to
follow up on, it can be challenging to manage the process efficiently and
effectively. That's why it's essential to streamline your follow-up process to achieve
better results.
Follow-up made simple involves creating a system that allows you to stay
organized, efficient, and effective in your follow-up efforts. This includes
implementing automation tools, creating a follow-up calendar, and utilizing
templates to save time and ensure consistency in your messaging.
By automating certain aspects of your follow-up process, you can save valuable
time and resources. For example, automated email campaigns can help you stay
top of mind with clients and provide them with valuable information without
requiring constant manual effort. This allows you to focus on more high-value
tasks, such as personalizing your follow-up efforts and engaging with clients.
Creating a follow-up calendar is also critical for streamlining your follow-up

process. By scheduling follow-up tasks in advance, you can ensure that you are

staying on top of your follow-up efforts and not missing any critical deadlines. This

can also help you avoid becoming overwhelmed by too many tasks at once and

allow you to plan your time more effectively.

Templates are another powerful tool for simplifying your follow-up process. By

creating templates for common follow-up messages, you can save time and

ensure consistency in your messaging. This also helps to ensure that you are

providing value to clients by including relevant and personalized information in

your follow-up messages.

In addition to these tactics, it's also essential to continuously evaluate and

optimize your follow-up process. By tracking metrics and analyzing data, you can

identify areas where your follow-up process could be improved and make changes

to achieve better results.

Overall, follow-up made simple involves creating a system that allows you to stay

organized, efficient, and effective in your follow-up efforts. By leveraging

automation tools, creating a follow-up calendar, and utilizing templates, you can

save valuable time and ensure consistency in your messaging. With a commitment

to simplifying your follow-up process and continuously optimizing your efforts, you
can build lasting relationships with clients, close more deals, and drive success for
your business.

The Benefits of Follow-Up: Improving Customer Retention and Driving Growth.

Follow-up is a crucial element of any successful real estate business. It's a critical
step in building strong relationships with clients, closing deals, and driving growth.
Effective follow-up strategies can help you retain customers and generate new
business opportunities, leading to increased revenue and a more successful
business.
One of the main benefits of follow-up is improving customer retention. Following

up with clients after a sale or transaction shows that you value their business and
care about their experience. This can lead to increased customer loyalty, repeat
business, and referrals. By maintaining regular contact with clients, you can stay
top of mind and continue to provide value to them, even after the transaction is
complete.
Another benefit of follow-up is driving growth. By staying in touch with clients and
providing valuable information and resources, you can position yourself as a
trusted advisor and thought leader in the industry. This can lead to new business
opportunities, as clients refer you to their friends, family, and colleagues.
Additionally, effective follow-up strategies can help you identify new leads and
nurture them through the sales funnel, ultimately leading to more closed deals and
increased revenue.
In addition to these benefits, follow-up can also help you improve customer
satisfaction and reduce churn. By regularly checking in with clients, you can
identify and address any issues or concerns they may have, preventing them from
becoming dissatisfied with your services and looking elsewhere for their real
estate needs.

Overall, the benefits of follow-up are clear. Effective follow-up strategies can
improve customer retention, drive growth, improve customer satisfaction, and
reduce churn. By prioritizing follow-up in your real estate business and
implementing effective strategies to stay in touch with clients, you can build strong
relationships, close more deals, and achieve greater success.

CHAPTER EIGHT

NEGOTIATION AND CLOSING THE DEAL.

Introduction to Negotiation and Closing the Deal: Understanding the Importance of Effective Communication

Effective communication is critical in any business negotiation, and in real estate,
it can make or break a deal. Successful real estate transactions require the ability
to communicate clearly and effectively, both with clients and other professionals in
the industry. This is especially important when it comes to negotiation and closing
deals.

In the world of real estate, negotiation is a key skill that can mean the difference
between a profitable sale and a missed opportunity. Negotiation involves finding
common ground with other parties, understanding their needs and priorities, and
working collaboratively to reach a mutually beneficial agreement. This process
requires effective communication, which involves not only the ability to articulate
your own needs and goals clearly but also the ability to listen actively and respond
thoughtfully to the needs and concerns of others.
In addition to effective communication, successful negotiation and deal closing in
real estate also requires a strong understanding of market trends and conditions,
knowledge of local regulations and laws, and the ability to think creatively to find
solutions to complex problems. By taking the time to prepare for negotiations,
understand the needs and priorities of all parties involved, and communicate
effectively, real estate professionals can increase their chances of closing deals
and building long-term relationships with clients and colleagues in the industry.

The Art of Negotiation: Key Strategies for Achieving a Win-Win Outcome

Negotiation is both an art and a science, and mastering the art of negotiation is a
critical skill for success in the real estate industry. Whether negotiating with
clients, contractors, or other industry professionals, real estate professionals need
to be able to find common ground and reach agreements that benefit all parties
involved. To do this, they must be equipped with a range of key negotiation
strategies.
One of the most important negotiation strategies is the ability to understand the
other party's perspective. Real estate professionals must be able to empathize
with the other party's needs and priorities and be willing to work collaboratively to
find mutually beneficial solutions. Active listening is a key component of
this strategy, as it allows negotiators to pick up on subtle cues and signals that
can help them understand the other party's motivations.

Another key negotiation strategy is the ability to set clear objectives and priorities.
This involves identifying what is most important to you and your client and being
willing to prioritize those objectives over other considerations. Effective
negotiators also understand the importance of building rapport and trust with the
other party, as this can help to create a more positive and collaborative negotiating
environment.
In addition to these strategies, successful negotiators in real estate must also be
prepared to think creatively and outside of the box. This can involve identifying
alternative solutions and compromises that may not have been initially considered,
or finding ways to reframe the negotiation to create a more positive outcome for
all parties involved.
Overall, the art of negotiation in real estate involves a combination of empathy,
active listening, clear communication, setting priorities, building trust, and creative
problem-solving. By mastering these strategies, real estate professionals can
achieve win-win outcomes that benefit everyone involved, and build strong and
lasting relationships with clients and colleagues in the industry.

Preparing for Success: Essential Steps to Take Before Entering a Negotiation

When it comes to negotiation, preparation is key. Before entering into any
negotiation, it's important to take the time to do your research and gather as much
information as possible about the other party and the situation at hand. This
includes understanding their goals, priorities, and potential objections, as well as
having a clear understanding of your own goals and limits.

One essential step in preparing for a successful negotiation is to establish your
BATNA, or Best Alternative To a Negotiated Agreement. This means identifying
what your options are if the negotiation falls through and you're unable to reach an
agreement. By having a clear understanding of your BATNA, you can ensure that

you're negotiating from a position of strength and avoid settling for a deal that isn't
in your best interest.
Another important aspect of preparation is considering the other party's
perspective and potential objections. This involves putting yourself in their shoes
and anticipating any concerns they may have. By understanding their perspective
and being able to address their concerns, you can build rapport and increase the
likelihood of reaching a mutually beneficial agreement.
Finally, it's important to prepare your negotiation strategy, including your opening
offer, potential concessions, and the tactics you'll use to achieve your goals. By
having a well-planned strategy and being prepared to adapt as needed, you can
increase your chances of success and achieve a favorable outcome in your
negotiations.

Navigating the Negotiation Process: Tips and Techniques for Effective Communication

Navigating the negotiation process requires effective communication skills that
help you articulate your needs and interests while also understanding the other
party's position. This involves active listening, asking the right questions, and
clarifying misunderstandings to ensure a shared understanding of the situation.
It's important to remain calm and composed throughout the process and avoid
getting defensive or confrontational, as this can hinder progress.
Effective negotiation also involves being able to identify areas of common ground
and using them to build consensus. This requires a certain level of flexibility and
willingness to compromise on less important issues to achieve a win-win
outcome. Negotiation is not about winning or losing, but rather finding a solution

that works for both parties.

In real estate negotiations, it's important to have a clear understanding of the

property and its value, as well as any legal or financial considerations that may

affect the negotiation. Doing your research beforehand and having a solid

understanding the market and comparable properties can give you an edge in

the negotiation process.

Ultimately, effective communication and a willingness to find common ground are

key to successfully navigating the negotiation process and achieving a mutually

beneficial outcome.

The Power of Persuasion: Leveraging Influence and Building Trust In Negotiations

Negotiations involve not only communication but also persuasion. The ability to

persuade effectively can make the difference between a successful negotiation

and a failed one. Persuasion involves building trust and leveraging influence to

achieve your desired outcome. In the context of real estate negotiations, this can
mean establishing credibility and demonstrating expertise in the market to gain
the trust of the other party. It can also mean finding common ground and
understanding the needs and motivations of both parties to reach a mutually
beneficial agreement.
To leverage influence effectively, negotiators must understand the power
dynamics at play and use them to their advantage. This can mean establishing a
sense of urgency or scarcity to create pressure for the other party to act or
presenting compelling data and arguments to support your position. However, it's
important to avoid using unethical or manipulative tactics, as this can damage
relationships and undermine trust.
Building trust is also a crucial component of effective persuasion. This can be
achieved by demonstrating honesty, integrity, and transparency throughout the
negotiation process. It can also mean being willing to make concessions or
compromises to show a commitment to finding a mutually beneficial agreement.
Ultimately, the power of persuasion is about creating a sense of collaboration and

working towards a shared goal. By leveraging influence and building trust,
negotiators can achieve their desired outcomes while also fostering long-term
relationships with the other party.

The Final Steps: Techniques for Closing the Deal and Ensuring a Successful Outcome

Closing a deal is one of the most crucial stages in any negotiation process,
especially in the real estate industry where big investments are involved. It is the
point where all parties involved in the negotiation have to come to a consensus
and finalize the agreement. Therefore, it is essential to have effective techniques
for closing a deal and ensuring a successful outcome.
One of the most important techniques for closing a deal is to clearly define the
terms and conditions of the agreement. This involves laying out all the key details,

such as the price, payment terms, contingencies, and other relevant factors. This
ensures that all parties involved have a clear understanding of what they are
agreeing to, and minimizes the chances of any misunderstandings or
disagreements arising in the future.
Another key technique for closing a deal is to be prepared to make compromises.
Negotiations often involve a certain amount of give and take, and it is important to
be flexible and open to making concessions to ensure that the deal can be closed.
This requires a willingness to listen to the other party's needs and concerns, and to
be creative in finding mutually beneficial solutions.
Building rapport and trust is also crucial when it comes to closing a deal. By
establishing a good relationship with the other party, and showing that you are
trustworthy and reliable, you can increase the likelihood of the deal being finalized.
This can involve taking the time to get to know the other party, being responsive
and communicative throughout the negotiation process, and following through on
any commitments made.
Finally, having a clear plan of action for closing the deal is essential. This involves
setting specific goals and timelines, and taking the necessary steps to ensure that

all parties are on the same page. This can include preparing all the necessary
documents and paperwork, coordinating with other professionals involved in the
process, and ensuring that all the relevant legal and regulatory requirements are
met.

In summary, closing a deal requires a combination of effective communication,
negotiation skills, trust-building, and strategic planning. By mastering these
techniques, real estate professionals can ensure that they can close deals
successfully and build long-term relationships with clients and partners.

Negotiating in Real Estate: Unique Considerations and Strategies for Success

When it comes to real estate negotiations, some unique considerations and strategies come into play. Real estate transactions involve significant amounts of money, intricate legal processes, and complex relationships between buyers, sellers, and agents. To navigate these complexities, it's crucial to have a thorough understanding of the industry and the specific deal you're working on.

One of the key considerations in real estate negotiations is market conditions. Understanding the current state of the market can help you determine the best approach to take when negotiating with buyers or sellers. For example, if it's a seller's market with high demand and low supply, buyers may need to be more flexible in their negotiations to secure a property. On the other hand, in a buyer's market with more supply than demand, sellers may need to be more open to negotiating on price and other terms.

Another important consideration in real estate negotiations is the legal and regulatory framework. Real estate transactions are subject to a variety of laws and regulations, from zoning and land use regulations to fair housing laws and disclosure requirements. Failing to comply with these regulations can lead to legal trouble and financial penalties, so it's important to work with a knowledgeable agent or attorney who can guide you through the process.

Effective communication is also essential in real estate negotiations. Clear, honest, and timely communication between all parties involved in a transaction can help build trust and reduce the likelihood of misunderstandings or disputes. Listening carefully to the other party's needs and concerns and being willing to compromise can also help you reach a mutually beneficial agreement.

Finally, real estate negotiations often involve emotional factors that can influence decision-making. For example, sellers may be emotionally attached to their property and reluctant to let it go for less than they feel it's worth, while buyers may be eager to secure a property they've fallen in love with. Recognizing and understanding these emotional factors can help you navigate negotiations more effectively and reach a successful outcome. Overall, successful real estate negotiations require a combination of market knowledge, legal expertise, effective communication, and emotional intelligence. By understanding the unique considerations and strategies involved in real estate negotiations, you can increase your chances of closing a deal that benefits all parties involved.

Overcoming Common Challenges in Negotiation and Deal Closing

Overcoming common challenges in negotiation and deal closing is crucial for success in real estate. Negotiation requires a set of skills that are unique to each individual and every transaction, and it is important to be prepared for the unexpectod. Some common challenges that arise during the negotiation and deal closing include conflicting interests, miscommunication, emotional attachments, and power imbalances.

To overcome these challenges, it is essential to have a clear understanding of your goals and priorities, as well

as the needs and motivations of the other party.
Effective communication and active listening are key to building trust and finding common ground. Emotions can run high during negotiations, so it is important to remain calm and level-headed while still being assertive. Additionally, it is important to be aware of power imbalances and to work towards creating a mutually beneficial outcome. This can involve finding creative solutions, such as offering concessions or exploring alternative options.

Another important aspect of overcoming challenges in negotiation and deal closing is to have a solid understanding of the legal and financial aspects of the transaction. This includes having a clear understanding of the terms of the contract, as well as any potential risks or liabilities.

Overall, by being proactive and prepared, communicating effectively, and finding creative solutions, it is possible to overcome common challenges in negotiation and deal closing and achieve a successful outcome in real estate transactions.

Building Long-Term Relationships: How Effective Negotiation Can Lead to Future Success

In the competitive world of real estate, building long-term relationships is crucial for success. Effective negotiation plays a key role in developing and maintaining these relationships. By prioritizing the needs and goals of all parties involved, a skilled negotiator can build trust and establish a foundation for future collaboration.

Effective negotiation involves more than just closing a deal - it requires a deep understanding of the unique needs and concerns of all parties involved. By taking the time to listen and understand each party's goals and priorities, a negotiator can develop creative solutions that meet everyone's needs. This approach not only leads to a successful deal but also establishes a foundation for future collaborations.

Furthormore, effective communication throughout the negotiation procoss is essential for bullding long term relationships. Clear and transparent communicatlon builds trust and minimizes misunderstandings that can damage relationships. By actively listening to all parties involved and communicating expectations and progress, a negotiator can establish a foundation of trust that can extend far beyond the current deal.

By building long-term relationships through effective negotiation, real estate professionals can establish a loyal client base and a strong network of industry contacts. These relationships can lead to future opportunities, referrals, and a competitive advantage in the market.

In summary, effective negotiation is not just about closing deals but also about building long-term relationships that can lead to future success. By prioritizing the needs and goals of all parties involved, communicating clearly and transparently, and taking a collaborative approach, real estate professionals can establish a foundation of trust and build relationships that can last for years to come.

Continuous Improvement: Strategies for Honing Your Negotiation and Closing Skills

Continuous improvement is a vital aspect of success in any field, especially in real estate. As such, honing your negotiation and closing skills is an ongoing process that requires dedication and commitment. To stay ahead of the curve and continue to improve your skills, it is important to develop effective strategies that can help you sharpen your skills and achieve better results.

One key strategy for continuous improvement is to seek feedback from others, such as clients, colleagues, or mentors. This feedback can help you identify areas for improvement and provide insights into how to enhance your negotiation and closing skills. Additionally, seeking out additional training and education in real estate can also help you stay up-to-date with the latest industry trends and best practices.

Another effective strategy is to stay organized and focused during negotiations. This includes preparing thoroughly beforehand, creating a clear plan and timeline, and staying calm and composed during the negotiation process. By maintaining a strategic mindset and focusing on the end goal, you can more effectively navigate the negotiation process and close deals successfully.

Additionally, building strong relationships with clients and colleagues can also contribute to continuous improvement in your negotiation and closing skills. By establishing trust and open communication, you can more effectively work together towards a common goal and build a foundation for future success.

Ultimately, continuous improvement requires a willingness to learn and adapt, as well as a commitment to ongoing self-reflection and self-evaluation. By developing effective strategies and continually seeking out opportunities for growth and development, you can hone your negotiation and closing skills and achieve greater success in the competitive world of real estate.

BONUS #1: 100+ SUCCESSFUL REAL ESTATE AGENT AFFIRMATIONS

- READ IT DAILY TO GET THE BEST RESULT

1. I am a successful real estate agent.
2. I am confident in my ability to help my clients buy or sell their homes.
3. I am a skilled negotiator and advocate for my clients.
4. attract clients who value my expertise and trust me to guide them through the
process.
5. I am constantly expanding my knowledge of the real estate industry.
6. I am always prepared and organized for every meeting and transaction.
7.
I have a deep understanding of my local real estate market.
8. I consistently exceed my client's expectations.
9. I am constantly setting and achieving new goals for my business.

10. I am committed to delivering exceptional customer service to every client.

11. Iam always networking and building relationships with other professionals in
the industry.

12. I am a master at marketing and promoting properties.

13. Iam able to adapt to changing market conditions and trends.

14. Iam a great listener and communicator with my clients.

15. I am passionate about helping people find their dream homes.

16. I am an expert at pricing properties accurately.

17. Iam always learning and growing as a real estate agent.

18. I am confident in my ability to handle any challenge that comes my way.

19. I am focused on achieving success for myself and my clients.

20. I am always looking for ways to improve my skills and knowledge.

21. I am grateful for the opportunity to help people buy or sell their homes.

22. I am a problem solver who can handle any situation that arises.

23. I am persistent and dedicated to achleving my goals.

24. I am a trusted advisor to my clients.

25. I am a skilled negotiator who always gets the best deal for my clients.

26. I am a master at creating and executing effective marketing strategies.

27. I am an expert in my field who constantly stays up-to-date on industry trends.

28. I am always professional and ethical in my dealings with clients.

29. I am a great listener who truly understands my clients' needs and desires.

30. I am a skilled communicator who can effectively convey information to clients.

31. I am a problem solver who can find creative solutions to any challenge.

32. I am a trusted advisor who always has my clients' best interests in mind.

33. I am always proactive and anticipating my clients' needs.

34. I am a master of time management and always prioritize my clients' needs.

35. I am an expert at navigating complex real estate transactions.

36. I am a skilled marketer who can promote properties to a wide audience.

37. I am an expert in my local real estate market who can help clients make
informed decisions.

38. I am a strategic thinker who can develop effective plans to achieve my goals.

39. I am a team player who works well with other professionals in the industry.

40. I am always looking for ways to innovate and improve my business.

41. I am a problem solver who can find solutions to any obstacle.
42. I am a skilled negotiator who can get the best deal for my clients.
43. I am a master at building and maintaining relationships with clients.
44. I am always looking for ways to go above and beyond for my clients.
45. I am a master of time management and always make the most of my time.
46. I am an expert in my local real estate market who can help clients make
informed decisions.
47. I am always seeking new opportunities for growth and success.
48. I am a visionary who can see the big picture and plan for the future.
49. I am always striving for excellence in everything I do.
50. I am a master at creating and executing effective business

BONUS #2: REAL ESTATE ADVERTISING STRATEGIES TO ENGAGE WITH THE TARGET AUDIENCE

In today's highly competitive real estate market, it's crucial to have effective advertising strategies that can engage with your target audience. With the right

advertising strategies, you can create brand awareness, generate leads, and

ultimately, drive sales. Here are some powerful and effective real estate

advertising strategies that can help you engage with your target audience:

1. Social media advertising: With the widespread use of social media platforms,

advertising on social media can be an effective way to reach your target

audience. By creating targeted social media ads, you can reach potential buyers

and sellers with specific demographics, interests, and behaviors.

2. Search engine marketing: Search engine marketing (SEM) involves placing ads

on search engine results pages (SERPs) based on keywords and phrases

related to real estate. With effective SEM campaigns, you can drive more traffic

to your website and generate more leads.

3. Content marketing: Content marketing involves creating informative and

engaging content that can attract and engage with your target audience. By

providing valuable content such as blog posts, infographics, and videos, you

can establish yourself as an expert in the real estate industry and build trust with potential clients.

4. Email marketing: Email marketing can be an effective way to reach out to
potential clients and keep them engaged with your business. By creating
targeted email campaigns, you can provide valuable information about
properties and keep your audience informed about your latest deals and
promotions.

5. Print advertising: Although digital marketing has become more prevalent in
recent years, traditional print advertising can still be effective in reaching
certain target audiences. By placing ads in local newspapers, magazines, and
real estate publications, you can reach potential clients who may not be as
active online.

6. Video marketing: Video marketing has become increasingly popular in recent
years, and for good reason. By creating engaging and informative videos about
properties, neighborhoods, and the real estate market, you can capture the
attention of potential clients and build your brand.

7. Referral marketing: Referral marketing involves encouraging your existing
clients to refer their friends and family to your business. By providing

exceptional service and asking for referrals, you can build a strong network of
loyal clients who can help you generate new business.
8. Event marketing: Hosting events such as open houses, the home buying seminars,
and charity events can be an effective way to engage with your target audience
in person. By providing valuable information and creating a positive experience,
you can build trust and establish yourself as a reputable real estate agent in
your community.
Utilizing these powerful real estate advertising strategies that can drive you to success by
maximizing your ROI and achieving your business goals.

BONUS #3: REAL ESTATE LISTING LEADS RESOURCES

As a real estate agent, one of the most important aspects of your business is
generating leads for potential clients. Real estate listing leads are particularly
valuable, as they represent clients who are actively looking to buy or sell a
property. However, finding and converting these leads can be a challenging task.

Here are some powerful and effective real estate listing lead resources that can
help you generate more leads and grow your business:
1. Online listing portals: Online listing portals such as Zillow, Redfin, and
Realtor.com are popular resource for buyers and sellers to search for
properties. As a real estate agent, you can leverage these portals to generate
leads by creating a profile, listing your properties, and responding to inquiries promptly.
2. Referral networks: Referral networks such as HomeLight and ReferralExchange
can connect you with other real estate agents and brokers who can refer
potential clients to you. By building relationships with other professionals in the
industry, you can expand your network and generate more leads.
3. Social media: Social media platforms such as Facebook, Twitter, and Instagram
can be powerful tools for generating real estate listing leads. By creating
targeted ads and content, engaging with your followers, and leveraging
hashtags, you can reach potential clients and build your brand.
4. Local events: Participating in local events such as home expos, trade shows,
and community events can be a great way to connect with potential clients

face-to-face. By providing valuable information, answering questions, and
building relationships, you can generate more leads and establish yourself as a
trusted real estate agent in your Community.
5. Direct mail: Although it may seem old-fashioned, direct mail can still be an
effective way to generate real estate listing leads. By sending targeted
postcards and flyers to specific neighborhoods or demographics, you can reach
potential clients who may not be as active online.
6. Networking events: Attending networking events such as industry conferences,
the local chamber of commerce meetings and other professional events can be a
great way to meet other real estate professionals and generate more leads.
7. Real estate lead generation companies: Real estate lead generation companies
such as Zurple and BoldLeads can provide you with pre-screened and qualified
leads that are ready to buy or sell. By working with these companies, you can
save time and resources on lead generation and focus on converting leads into
clients.
By leveraging these powerful real estate listing lead resources, you can generate
more leads, grow your business, and achieve your goals as a real estate agent.

Remember to continually test and refine your lead generation strategies to ensure
that you're maximizing your ROI and achieving the best possible results.

BONUS #4: REAL ESTATE COLD-CALLING TECHNIQUES THAT REALLY

WORK (WITH SCRIPT).....

As a real estate agent, one of the most effective ways to generate leads and grow
your business is through cold calling. Cold calling involves reaching out to
potential clients who may not be familiar with your services or in the market for a
property. However, with the right techniques and approach, cold calling can be a
highly successful way to generate new leads and expand your network. Here are
some powerful and effective real estate cold-calling techniques that really work,
along with a script to help you get started:
1. Research your leads: Before making a cold call, it's important to do your
research and learn as much as possible about the person or business you're

reaching out to. This will help you tailor your pitch and approach to their
specific needs and interests.
2. Build rapport: Building rapport is key to making a successful cold call. Start by
introducing yourself and your business, and ask open-ended questions to
engage the person in conversation. This will help you establish a connection
and build trust.
3. Focus on benefits, not features: When making your pitch, focus on the benefits
of working with you rather than just the features of your services. For example,
instead of simply listing the services you offer, explain how they can help the
person achieve their goals or solve a specific problem.
4. Use a script: While you don't want to come across as overly rehearsed or
robotic, having a script can help you stay focused and confident during a cold
call. Your script should include an introduction, a brief explanation of your
services, and a call to action.
5. Be persistent: Cold calling can be a numbers game, so it's important to be
persistent and keep making calls even if you don't immediately see results.
Remember that not everyone will be interested in your services, but with
enough persistence, you'll eventually find those who are.

Here's a sample cold-calling script that you can use as a starting point:
"Hi, my name is [Your Name] and I'm a real estate agent with [Your Company].
noticed that you recently [trigger event or interest, such as listed your property for
sale or expressed interest in buying a new home]. I wanted to reach out and see if I
could offer any assistance or answer any questions you might have. Our company
has a proven track record of helping clients [benefit, such as selling their home
quickly or finding their dream home], and I'd love to have the opportunity to work with
you. Would you be available for a brief call or meeting to discuss how we can help?
Thank you for your time, and I look forward to hearing back from you."

By implementing these powerful real estate cold calling techniques and using a
script as a guide, you can effectively engage potential clients, generate new leads,
and grow your real estate business.

BONUS #5: EFFECTIVE FOLLOW-UP METHOD & SCRIPTS FOR REALTORS

As a real estate agent, follow-up is an essential part of the sales process. Effective
follow-up not only helps you build stronger relationships with potential clients, but
it also increases the likelihood of closing a sale. However, many realtors struggle
with the right approach and scripts to use for follow-up. Here are some powerful
and effective follow-up methods and scripts for realtors:
1. Personalize your follow-up: Personalization is key when it comes to follow-up.
When following up with a potential client, make sure to reference specific
details from your previous conversation to show that you're invested and
attentive.
2. Use multiple channels: People have different communication preferences, so
it's important to use multiple channels for follow-up. This could include email,
phone calls, text messages, and social media.
3. Offer value: Follow-up isn't just about checking in, it's also about providing value
to the client. Consider sharing relevant articles or resources, offering a free
consultation, or providing updates on the local real estate market.

4. Use a script: While you don't want to sound overly rehearsed, having a script
can help you stay focused and confident during follow-up. Your script should
include a brief recap of your previous conversation, a reference to any action
items or next steps, and a call to action.
5. Be persistent: Following up once isn't enough. It's important to be persistent
and continue following up until you receive a definitive answer or the client
indicates that they're no longer interested.
Here's a sample follow-up script that you can use as a starting point:
"Hi [Client Name], it's [Your Name] from [Your Company]. I just wanted to follow up
on our previous conversation and see if you had any further questions or if there's
anything else I can do to assist you. As a reminder, we discussed [recap of
the previous conversation] and we talked about [specific action item or next steps]. I
wanted to make sure that you had all the information you need to make an
informed decision. If you're still interested in [specific service or property], I'd be
happy to provide more information or set up a time to discuss further. Let me
know what works best for you. Thank you for your time and I look forward to
hearing back from you."

By implementing these effective follow-up methods and using a script as a guide,
you can strengthen your relationships with potential clients, provide value, and
increase your chances of closing a sale.

CONCLUSION

As we come to the end of this real estate book, it's important to reflect on the
valuable insights and strategies that have been shared throughout these pages.
Whether you're a seasoned real estate professional or just starting in the
industry, there's something to be gained from the knowledge and experiences that
have been shared.
Throughout this book, we've explored a range of topics related to real estate, from
advertising strategies and lead generation to negotiation tactics and effective
communication. We've delved into the intricacies of the market, discussing trends
and insights that can help you make informed decisions when it comes to buying
or selling property. We've also examined the importance of building strong
relationships with clients and the critical role that communication and folloW-up
play in the sales process.

As a real estate agent, your success hinges on your ability to adapt and evolve in a
constantly changing market. By implementing the strategies and techniques
discussed in this book, you can stay ahead of the curve and position yourself for
long-term success. But ultimately, success in real estate is not just about the
tactics and strategies you use, but also about the relationships you build and the
values you uphold.
At its core, real estate is about helping people find the right property for their
needs and supporting them throughout the buying or selling process. It's about
providing value, building trust, and delivering exceptional service. So as you go out
into the world armed with the knowledge and insights from this book, remember to
keep these principles at the forefront of your approach.
In conclusion, I hope that the information shared in this book has been valuable to
you and that it has provided you with the tools and strategies you need to succeed
in the real estate industry. Remember to always stay curious, continue learning,
and above all, put the needs and interests of your clients first. With dedication,
hard work, and a commitment to excellence, you can achieve success as a real

estate agent and make a positive impact on the lives of those you serve.